CHAKRA HEALING BIBLE

5 in 1

The Complete Guide to Simple and Effective Self-Healing & Meditation
Techniques to Balance Your Chakras, Boost Your Positive Energy,
and Improve Your Psychic Abilities

Willow Kumar

TABLE OF CONTENTS

WHY CHAKRA HEALING BIBLE?

Chakra healing is a centuries-old therapy that is still used today to heal the soul, mind, and body. The energy centers in our bodies, known as chakras, have a significant impact on our overall health. Newcomers to this alternative type of spirituality can comprehend every part of chakra power through this finely crafted, five-in-one Chakra Healing Bible. This thorough guide covers each chakra, with its associated colors, therapeutic stone, and emotional and physical acts, in addition to an insightful introduction. The base, sacral, solar plexus, heart, throat, forehead, and crown chakras, plus a few recently found chakras from various traditions, should all be worked on one at a time. There is also valuable information on how to use yoga poses and meditations to develop each chakra, as well as connections between chakras and energy healing methods.

Perhaps there is a whole science working behind the core concept of Chakras and their function. This *Chakra Healing Bible* is your one-stop shop to learn everything related to chakras. In this all-in-one package, there are five books, with each book explaining a different aspect of chakra healing therapy. Book 1 is written to give you a detailed overview of what Chakras are and what you should know about them. The second book is all about therapeutic meditation and yoga poses. Book 3 gives you practical ideas to heal your chakras through various home remedies and treatments. All the daily and seasonal rituals are encompassed in Book 4, whereas Book 5 discusses what chakra healing is like in the modern digital age.

BOOK 1:
CHAKRA OVERVIEW

"What lies behind us and what lies before us are tiny matters compared to what lies within us."

—Henry Stanley Haskins

The road to peace, strength, courage, and confidence all starts from within us. It is often the fight within that makes us successful and content on the outside. The concept of healing through chakras is derived from the same ideology; it introduces us to the powers and energies which reside inside of us and makes us use them to heal our mind, emotions, and body. Chakra systems are centuries old. They are not connected to one single religion or faith; rather, they are now considered part of the collective understanding of the human body, which helps us to understand the energies present inside and outside of our body. Because there are several chakras and different systems, it's crucial to understand that each chakra has a distinct color, shape, name, and position in the body. According to old traditions, there are seven chakras, each of which is a part of our energetic being and is situated in a vital part of the body. Imagine the chakras as energy wheels that are constantly rotating to produce a combination of energy and life force. The root chakra, which is present at the base of the body, connects to the crown chakra, which is present at the top of the head, and beyond. Life is beautiful when the chakras are in harmony and functioning smoothly. We feel a sense of completeness in our minds, bodies, and souls. Our interactions, discussions, actions, objectives, and interests all affect the flow of energy through our bodies. A healthy chakra system can be compared to cool water flowing down a stream: it touches everything it comes in contact with while moving along its path with grace and fluidity.

Life can be difficult when the chakras are out of balance, with some being overactive and others underactive. If you peel away a layer or two, you may not immediately see this misalignment, but you'll soon see where work needs to be done. The chakra system is internal and invisible, which is why if any of the chakras are out of balance, the only way to identify them is through symptoms. According to the chakra concept, there is a peaceful, subtle body, also known as the energetic body, which consists of the seven chakras. It is something that we always feel but cannot see or touch. It is the part of us that beats our heart and has gut instincts, and the energy within us that moves, connects, and forms our existence are all examples of this.

Energies around and within us matter, as they are constantly affecting our surroundings. What we give out into the universe turns or comes back to us, so it is important to not only understand the different chakras that are present within us but also to identify when they are blocked and ways to heal them through meditation, yoga, and physical activities. For someone who hasn't been introduced to the whole "chakra healing" concept, it can be a little too much to absorb at once. I went through something similar when a friend of mine first introduced me to it, but once I had read about it in depth, it started to make more sense. That is why here, in this book, I am going unveil all the different types of chakras and what effects blocking and unblocking those chakras bring upon us.

UNDERSTANDING CHAKRAS

Root Chakra
Basic Trust

Sacral Chakra
Sexuality, Creativity

Solar Chakra
Wisdom, Power

Heart Chakra
Love, Healing

Throat Chakra
Communication

Third Eye
Awareness

Crown Chakra
Spirituality

"Chakras." You must have heard your favorite yoga teacher or some yogi on the television or Internet talk about them, and you must have seen promises of chakra balancing in everything from beautiful stones to essential oils. But what exactly are they? What does having an imbalance or blocked chakra mean?

Chakra is basically a Sanskrit word that translates into "wheel" or "disc." Imagine the chakras as pranic energy wheels that start at the base of your spine and are positioned at various points as they travel upward. The seventh chakra, which is located on the crown of your head, is the last of the seven chakras. An eighth chakra, though it is not usually discussed in the traditional seven-chakra models, also exists. Today, chakras are typically defined as force centers within the physical body. The chakras are connected to different spinal centers and the physiological organ systems, such as digestion, respiration, and reproduction, that they control. Each chakra has a unique name, color, stone and crystal association, and energetic domain that it governs.

I prefer to see each chakra as a tiny computer that is programmed to carry out specific functions that support our feelings, ideas, and personal development. Chakra balancing can help when those computers need to be reprogrammed to move us in the right way. Chakra balancing restores energy flow to its normal, balanced state. I enjoy using chakra meditation as a part of my yoga practice, where I concentrate on the chakra's color, chant mantras, meditate using yantras, use chakra affirmations, and occasionally employ chakra gems and stones to restore balance.

History of Chakra Systems

The Vedas, some of the most ancient religious writings in existence, contain the earliest references to chakras. Scholars assert that oral tradition was the primary method by which knowledge of the chakra system was initially transmitted to each succeeding generation. This was carried out by Indo-Europeans, also referred to as Aryans. The precise date when this occurred is unknown. However, we do know that between 1500 and 500 BCE, the chakra system was initially discovered in Vedic scriptures in ancient India. Each Veda has four subdivisions, and one of these, the Upanishads, deals with Hindu spirituality, philosophy, and meditation. The earliest texts described chakras. The subsequent Upanishads, however, provided stronger proof of the chakras' genesis.

The initial spelling of "chakra" was "cakra." Its meaning is "wheel" or "disc." According to some scholars, they did not refer to chakras as "spinning discs of energy"—nothing like how we define things now. They were also not connected to subtle body components like kundalini or the life force, known as prana. Instead, some academics assert that the term "chakra" may have first been used to describe the cakravartins, or chariot wheels, of kings. Even now, only four of the five chakras are used in the majority of Buddhist tantric schools, known as Vajrayana. The five chakras, which are prevalent in many forms of Buddhism, are:

- Genital
- Navel
- Heart
- Throat
- Crown

The solar plexus and sacral chakras are located in the genitalia and the navel, respectively. The root and crown chakras are the only two missing from the contemporary seven-chakra system. Many academics think that the second chakra is a combination of the root and genital or sacral chakras. The third eye chakra is also a part of the crown chakra. Numerous Buddhist and Hindu gurus were more engaged in the technique and imagery of the subtle body and chakras, which is one of the causes of the numerous variances.

Without talking about Buddhist tantra and other Tibetan and esoteric Buddhist rituals, one cannot explain the history of chakras. However, it's crucial to distinguish them from the conventional Indian and Hindu chakra systems. The hues of the rainbow are not related to the original chakra system. This was a contemporary, Western, and New Age creation. Christopher Hills made the initial discovery that the chakras correspond to the light spectrum and rainbow colors and discussed it in his 1977 book, *Nuclear Evolution*. Instead, the chakras are linked to one of the five main elements through the Sanskrit Bija mantras. For instance, LAM consistently links to the earth element. The earth element typically has a connection to the root chakra. This isn't always the case, though! Element associations with various chakras are also possible in the classical Hindu chakra system. For instance, the wind element is generally linked to the heart chakra. However, some tantric lineages have also connected the earth element with the heart chakra.

In the 1880s, the idea of a system of seven chakras was introduced to the West; at the time, each chakra was connected to a certain nerve plexus. Sir John Woodroffe, also known as Arthur Avalon, translated the *a-Cakra-Nirpaa* and the *Pduk-Pacaka*, two Indian books, in 1918 and popularized the seven-chakra system in the West with his book *The Serpent Power*. The tradition of each of the seven chakras being related to an endocrine gland dates back to the 1920s. The bottom six chakras have more recently been connected to glands and nerve plexuses. Leadbeater added the seven colors of the rainbow in 1927; a different scheme from the 1930s called for six colors plus white. The chakra system with rainbow colors that is most popular now was invented in *Nuclear Evolution*. Hills' book is also among the most important contemporary texts for understanding the beginnings and development of chakras.

The Healing of Chakras

Chakra knowledge is considered to be ancient wisdom that has been practiced for ages in many ancient societies. Chakras have attracted greater attention recently since we are beginning to sense that simply concentrating on our physical health is not delivering us complete wellness. Despite numerous medical advancements, something still seems to be wrong or missing, despite our best efforts to identify it. I think we as a society are beginning to comprehend that other variables may be influencing our present health issues in some way, even if we don't know how. What if you discovered that most physical symptoms we encounter—aside from incidents like automobile accidents and other types of direct physical trauma—could be avoided because they often represent unresolved issues in the energies within our body? The chakras! Our lives are in total harmony, and our health is good when our chakras are balanced. We will eventually experience emotional distress or illness if a chakra becomes blocked. Because everything is energy, when we take care of and maintain the health of our energy bodies through techniques like acupuncture, Reiki, meditation, yoga, and qi gong, we resolve problems before they manifest in the physical body.

The Flow of "Life Energy": Prana

According to Chakra scholars, there is a subtle life force energy that forms the basis of all life and the entire universe, and this energy runs through us. Most yogis have experienced prana, the subtle energy that circulates through our bodies that you cannot see, touch, or taste. This ethereal force permeates our bodies and drives every action we do, from large-scale physical movements to minute biochemical reactions. The goal of many yoga movements is to keep that energy flowing into and out of our bodies.

The 3,000-year-old Chandogya Upanishad text is the first to use the Sanskrit word prana, which was then elaborated upon and detailed in succeeding Upanishads. The prana and the energetic anatomy that sustains it was further developed in the classical books of Ayurveda, tantra yoga, and hatha yoga. "Life force energy," "breath of life," "vital energy," "spirit energy," or "vital principle" are all translations of the Sanskrit term "*prana*." In yogic teachings, this phrase is used to generally refer to the universe's manifest energy. This innate creative force is always at work both inside and outside of us. The breath is usually discussed in yoga's breathing exercises because it is thought to be the most subtle form of prana in our bodies. In addition to creating the energy of our mind, prana controls all bodily processes.

Purpose of Prana

The source of all bodily activity is prana. The food we eat, the liquid we drink, the air we inhale, and the energy of the earth and sky that we absorb all contribute to the entry of prana into our body. Every cell in the body receives prana through thousands of small passageways called nadis. Think of this as a "life-energy circulation system" in the body, in which nadis are like blood vessels, prana is like blood, and chakras are the organs that receive and release prana. The Ida, Pingala, and Sushumna are the body's three principal nadis; they all originate near the base of the spine and continue upward to the head. While the Sushumna goes straight up the spine to the crown of the head, the other nadis (Ida and Pingala) spiral upward and connect to opposing nostrils. The Ida, Pingala, and Sushumna all cross one other and intersect at the location of the chakras. The distribution and flow of prana throughout the entire body are controlled by the chakras, which are connected to the tens of thousands of tiny nadis. When any of the chakras is blocked in the body, it breaks the flow of prana, which negatively affects our mind, body, and energies around us.

All of our conscious and unconscious biological processes, including breathing, digestion, blood flow, urination, and cellular growth and healing, are governed by it. The capacity of the nadis and the chakras determine how the prana flow distributes energy throughout the body. Moreover, the quality of our ideas, emotions, and consciousness are animated and impacted by prana. The amount and flow of prana in our bodies directly affect our general health and well-being. The impact of shakti, a denser variation of universal energy, on our physical selves and surroundings is even greater. The latent spiritual energy that is curled up at the base of the spine is known as kundalini. Kundalini, one kind of shakti energy, is a reservoir of dormant energy that can only be roused through rigorous yoga practice. Shiva, the energy of all consciousness, is the opposing power to shakti.

Flow of Prana

Our vital energy moves in relation to how our bodies move and are positioned. For instance, if you hunch over, the passage of prana through your body is reduced, and your breathing and energy channels are restricted. The flow of your prana will therefore be dulled and restricted if you have bad posture. Energy tends to move toward your head as you stand up. Your energy moves downward toward your feet as you sit down. The breath is also linked to the movement of our life force. Energy is drawn higher during inhalation and flows downward during exhalation. You will experience more of the sensation of standing if you associate inhaling with standing and exhaling with sitting.

Now, if you think about all the breathing exercises, the different yoga and meditation postures that experts talk about, they are actually used to keep prana flowing through the body. Yoga was, in fact, created to channel, generate, let energy flow up the "Sushumna" nadi to the crown chakra, as well as to circulate, cultivate, and govern prana. Asana yoga strengthens the nadis and cultivates and circulates the body's vitality. Using different breathing techniques, or pranayama, the nadis are cleansed while controlling and cultivating the vital force. Bandhas are dynamic locks that focus the prana in the three primary nadis and contain it in the torso. Mudras control prana, direct it into the chakras, and awaken the kundalini shakti.

Balancing of Chakras

Energy healing, called chakra balancing, focuses on directing energy into the seven chakras. When we discuss chakra treatment, we're speaking about energy body treatment; the body is made up of more than only the physical body. Through the use of crystals, essential oil blends, massage, and energetic techniques, the therapy seeks to uncover any potential blockages in the client. The goal is to remove any chakra blockages and encourage a free flow of energy to reestablish equilibrium and a sensation of well-being. You may be able to do the following by balancing your chakras:

- Maintain your composure in daily life
- Recognize difficulties for what they are and resist their influence
- Get past any experiences from your past that might have affected you
- Assist others without letting their issues affect you
- Enhance your self-esteem, vitality, freedom, and happiness to feel positive about life and yourself every day

How you feel and interact with conditions in your life depends on the condition of your chakras and energy field. With the help of this activity, we may take care of our consciousness and discover the lessons we are meant to learn before they show up as disease or loss. Chakras that are in balance promote both mental and emotional health. Numerous benefits result from altered energy patterns, such as:

MYTHS ABOUT CHAKRA HEALING

In order to understand the chakra healing process, it is important to free your mind from pre-existing misconceptions about it. Since the systems have been in existence for centuries, many myths and rumors have been attached to chakras over the years, but none of them are true; rather, most of the myths are contrary to the actual concepts. So, let me just burst a few of the chakra healing myths for you to clear your mind; then I will explain the chakra systems:

Myth 1: The chakras are "things" that are located somewhere in the body, possibly in the glands, nerve plexuses, or the spine. The chakras are obviously not physical objects, but those of us who are literal thinkers may not have considered what this means. We continue to talk about chakras as if they are just organs, like the liver or spleen, or as if an autopsy would reveal a series of different-colored lotuses running through the middle of the torso. It is preferable to think of a chakra as the meeting place of the main energy channels (nadis) in a level of awareness, which causes psychosomatic sensations and functions and can be used as a focus for spiritual practice and meditation. So, they are energy centers that are not physically visible, but they are hypothesized to be present at different spots in the body, according to the role they play in controlling our spiritual energies.

Myth 2: The rainbow colors represent the seven chakras. Tempting! But regrettably, the primary texts about chakra make no mention of rainbows. Several writings explain various colors (or, often, no color at all). The navel center lotus, for instance, has been described as being black, dark green, dark blue, golden, or red. The chakra associations are a visualization technique, not a description of the physical world.

The Adhara lotus (the second Muladhara chakra) has a red Dakini Devi, a yellow pericarp, and four crimson petals with gold Sanskrit characters. There is a vermilion lotus and lightning-colored letters on the Svadhishthana chakra. Its deity Hari is blue but dressed in yellow, and the blue goddess Rakini is seated on a red lotus in the brilliantly white pericarp. The letters are a beautiful blue tint, the pericarp is crimson, and the Manipura lotus is the color of a rain cloud. The shakti lakini is blue and sits on a crimson lotus, while Rudra, the deity of the place, is red but appears white due to ashes.

A visualization method that, it turns out, differs depending on religion includes assigning colors to the chakras. Attributes are not describing reality in the physical world; rather, they are for practice with a specific goal or consequence.

Myth 3: Chakra repair requires outside work. It is true that you may need some outside help to introduce yourself to chakras and ways to heal them. But ultimately, you are the one who cures yourself, not someone else. I always let people know this information. While healers can guide you on your path, personal healing is ultimately our responsibility. Everyone has different emotions, minds, and bodies; their chakra healing is connected to how they see themselves and what they are doing to heal.

Myth 4: A particular faith is associated with chakra healing. Although religious writings served as the chakra system's primary roots, it has subsequently evolved to encompass a wider knowledge and practice that is today accepted by individuals from all walks of life. Chakra health has grown to be a significant practice for many people on spiritual journeys, unrelated to religion.

Myth 5: Chakra therapy is a type of dark or demonic ritual. When done correctly, true chakra healing is utterly the opposite of demonic. Your body, mind, spirit, and heart are all receiving light, awareness, and consciousness from you, which chases away the dark demonic shadows.

Myth 6: There are seven chakras. According to different religious findings and studies, there are more than the basic seven chakras we hear about. *Nath Charit* shows 12 chakras, four of which are located between the two-petaled lotus at the base of the eyebrow and the many-petaled lotus above the crown of the head. Nine chakras are described in Gorakshanatha's *Siddha-Siddhanta-Paddhati.* Six are described in the *Netra Tantra* (pelvic floor, navel, heart, palate, eyebrow, and crown), albeit they go by different names than the system that is most popular today. Famous Kashmiri tantric master Abhinavagupta speaks of a five-chakra system that includes the base, Kanda (pelvis), heart, palate, and crown. Twelve chakras are also mentioned in the influential Shaiva scripture, the *Vijnana Bhairava Tantra.*

There are other systems that variously define three, four, five, nine, eleven, or twelve major centers. The "6 + 1" system, which is currently prominent (the root, pelvis, navel, heart, throat, and eyebrow centers, plus one at the top of the head), is just one of them. There are actually countless energy centers throughout the body, but only twelve major ones run along the central axis. Minor energy centers are known as marma points in Ayurveda, whereas centers that are aligned with the body's axis are known as chakras. Why are there so many various systems? The number of centers listed and explained varies depending on the custom or practice. Different schools of thought or books employ various conceptual frameworks to suggest or outline visualizations, behaviors, and power invocations (deities). For instance, some traditions place more emphasis on the Talu chakra, located at the soft palate, while others completely ignore it. Some traditions focus just on the navel or pelvis, the heart, and brain regions, while others have extensive rituals for six or more chakras.

How to Know your Chakra is Blocked?

The truth is that you can't know for sure that your chakra is blocked by simply measuring your body temperature like you do when you are down with fever or influenza. Many people experience chakra blockage in many different ways. Sometimes a blockage is accompanied by bodily symptoms, and other times it is accompanied by emotional symptoms. I know, that's annoying to hear. It actually depends on the individual. There are Indian gurus who have practiced sadhana for countless years to develop otherworldly abilities, such as the ability to identify blocked chakras. Your intuition typically goes hand in hand with it. Your Sacral chakra may be blocked if you experience creative blockage—feeling as though your capacity to play and create is restrained. Your throat chakra may not be functioning properly if you feel unsure of what is true or where to direct your focus. Each chakra blockage manifests itself differently, and all the symptoms of blocked and unhealthy chakras are shared in detail in the "Are Your Chakras Balanced?" section of Book 2 of this *Chakra Healing Bible*.

How Long Does Chakra Balancing Take?

Sadly, there isn't simple response to this. Anyone who claims differently doesn't completely comprehend chakras. While some can complete intense yoga with a prescribed set of techniques and have their chakras freed within a week, some people can practice yoga for a lifetime and still have their chakras blocked. And once the chakra is opened, it may get blocked again after some time, as you keep experiencing various interactions and emotions. So, you can say that it is not a one-time thing or one-size-fits-all formula. You may find equilibrium day by day with perseverance and effort.

There are a few simple things you should keep in mind when you get started with chakra healing. Don't be too hard on yourself. Those who are only beginning to connect with their chakras usually lose patience with themselves very fast. If they don't see quick results, they usually start to think poorly of themselves. Please keep in mind that everyone is unique, that everyone's own unfolding follows a perfect timeline, and that everything, including your healing, is going precisely as it should. Whether chakra healing is practiced to resolve a particular problem or to achieve enlightenment is an internal investigation rather than an end in itself. Because of this, chakra healing is not something you can just "speed up," just like with physical healing. However, receiving healing services and using other methods can eliminate energetic sludge and harmonize your energy centers. It takes time for transformation. As you progress on this journey, be kind to yourself. Never force your energies or push yourself past your comfort zone. People usually push themselves past what is comfortable when they are eager to connect with their chakras. However, you might get a headache by doing so. Take a pause as soon as you begin to experience resistance. Ask for assistance from a healer when you need it. Although you may achieve a lot on your own, guidance can occasionally be beneficial, particularly if you feel like your healing process has reached a roadblock or the pain you are experiencing is negatively affecting your quality of life. If and when you decide to seek assistance, go to every length to check if the provider is certified or licensed in the modality you choose. Before scheduling an appointment, extensively investigate them.

How are Colors Related to Chakras?

You must have seen the rainbow-colored chart representing different chakras on the Internet. Those colors make you think about what colors have to do with chakras. Well, there is, in fact, a close relationship between colors and chakras. Remember how I explained chakras as energy centers that absorb or release the energy coming in and out of the body? It is said that the type of vibration or frequency that radiates through different chakras is different, and each frequency corresponds to a particular color on the light spectrum. For example, chakras associated with a violet color radiate energy with the same frequency as the violet part of white light does.

By knowing the colors associated with the chakras, we can use the same colors to unblock and heal the respective chakras.

CHAKRA SYMBOLS EXPLAINED

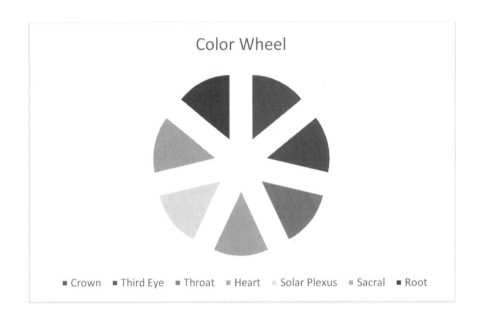

E very chakra sign serves as a reminder of our relationship with the divine. Yoga practice aids in our connection to the forces of the universe. Contrary to what Instagram portrays, yoga isn't simply about elegant arm balances on cliffs and propped-up, essential oil-infused restorative positions. Benefits to physical health and fitness are byproducts of the actual deal. Yoga is a huge science that allows us to connect with the cosmos by using the geometry of our own energy systems to bring our inner and outer worlds into harmony. In each chakra symbol, there are a few common components:

The sacred circle. Mandala and yantra are terms that are usually used interchangeably. Mandala is the Sanskrit word for "circle." Yantra means "any tool for holding or restricting" in English. These power diagrams are mostly made up of circles, squares, triangles, and lotus petals in the yogic tradition of sacred geometry. Moreover, they represent the wide universe or the energy field of a god in Hinduism. The circular shape symbolizes the idea that there is only one source of life force, which permeates everything and never ends. The practitioner's spiritual path, the unifying power of all life, and the necessity for each of us to find our unique position in the cosmos are all represented by the chakra symbols.

Inside and outside of the circle. A ubiquitous symbol for infinity, the circle is the endless and cyclical nature of energy. The geometric shape that unites all chakra symbols is the circle. Each chakra sign incorporates the circle to serve as a reminder of our relationship to the divine and as a symbol of unity and connection with ourselves, others, and a higher good.

The lotus flower. The lotus is another mystical, magical symbol that usually appears in chakra signs. This blossom is a symbol of our kinship with God, our unification with all life, and the prosperity and eternities of these vital links. The opening of our understanding is represented by the petals' outward-pointing appearance.

TYPES OF CHAKRAS

The seven-chakra system is the oldest and most commonly known system around the world. In this system, it is believed that there are seven centers of energy within the human body, and they run along the spine from top to bottom. To understand the power of chakras, modern-age chakra healing, and other related concepts, it is important to first understand what this system corresponds to:

Root Chakra (Muladhara)

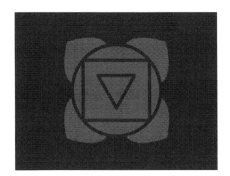

The first energy wheel starts at the base of your spine and is known as the root or Muladhara chakra. This chakra is related to the earth and directly to the depth, strength, and support of the roots we have established. The Muladhara chakra represents root or fundamental needs, including family, water, food, and shelter. We feel firmly planted, comfortable, and secure when this chakra is in balance. Our lives go smoothly along with steady vitality. Life is difficult when things are not in harmony. When we experience insecurity and fear, our survival mode activates. This may result in gaining weight, constipation, fatigue, depressive symptoms, anxiety, and stress. It has grounding energy and interacts with the earth's star chakra to instill a sense of stability. A person feels balanced, safe, and at peace with themselves and their surroundings when this chakra is open. Red is the hue that represents the root chakra. Spending lots of time in nature is one of the finest methods to increase the life force in the root chakra because it is associated with the earth element. Walking through a forest or climbing a mountain has strong grounding properties that help the mind and soul become quiet and clear, releasing fear and tension.

Location: Base of Spine

Element: Earth

Color: Red

Meaning: Stability

Symbol Components: The inverted triangle, an alchemical symbol for earth, is the element of this chakra, and it symbolizes drawing energy downwards. The first chakra's grounding force, which represents stability, is contained in the triangle. The square has four corners—the number four stands for a solid foundation and a sturdy building, and it represents that the rest of the chakras can be safely opened on the foundation of a balanced root chakra.

The root chakra lotus' four petals represent the four mental states of Manas (mind), Buddhi (intellect), Chitta (awareness), and Ahamkara (ego), as well as stability and organization. Because the root chakra is the base point, the four-petaled lotus as a whole represents the genesis of human consciousness.

Sacral Chakra (Svadhistana)

The second energy wheel, often known as the sacral chakra, is a representation of sexual and creative energy within the body. The lower belly is home to the sacral chakra, or Svadhistana in Sanskrit, which oversees the reproductive organs. The element of water is linked to the Svadhistana chakra. When we think of water, we picture its flexibility, freedom, and fluidity. In contrast to being overcome by emotions, a person with an open sacral chakra can go along with the twists and turns of life and find ease. The color of the second chakra is orange. Spend time around or in sizable pools of water, ideally from natural sources, to connect with the water element. Go swimming in the sea, kayaking on a lake, or canoeing down a river. As an alternative, taking baths can assist in opening this chakra. The power to be sexual, emotional, creative, and in tune with ourselves and others is what the second chakra is all about. Life gets full of abundance, creativity, movement, procreation, pleasure, and happy relationships when this chakra is balanced. You may feel emotional instability, apprehension about change, sexual dysfunction, depression, a lack of inspiration, persistent low-back discomfort, reproductive problems, and other lower-pelvic problems when you're out of alignment.

Location: Below Belly Button

Element: Water

Color: Orange

Meaning: Pleasure, creativity, and sexuality

Symbol Components: Six-Petalled Lotus. The six petals of this lotus are associated with qualities like anger, jealousy, cruelty, hatred, pride, and desire that must be overcome to purify Svadhisthana.

The Circles: The circles represent the cyclic reality of life: birth, death, and rebirth.

The Crescent Moon: It symbolizes the cycles of never-ending change, chaos, and constant movement.

Solar Plexus (Manipura Chakra)

The third wheel of energy, known as the Manipura or navel chakra, is linked to the element of fire. This chakra represents our personal power and is in charge of our digestion, metabolism, self-worth, and sense of who we are. Self-assurance, a sense of direction, and self-motivation are all present in your life when this chakra is balanced. You have the capacity to let go of problems as they arise and to remain detached from the current situation's external factors. You may feel digestive problems, low self-esteem, and trouble making decisions when you're out of harmony.

Location: The upper abdomen

Element: Fire

Color: Yellow

Meaning: Confidence and self-esteem

Symbol Components: Ten-Petalled Lotus. The solar plexus chakra's ten petals stand for the ten pranas that every one of us has. The ten pranas are essentially energy vibrations and currents.

The energy of the lower three chakras is concentrated and spins upward toward the higher chakras, as represented by the inverted triangle.

Heart (Anahata Chakra)

The heart chakra, which connects the three physical chakras with the three spiritual chakras, is the fourth wheel of energy. The fourth chakra can integrate and open by bringing the first three chakras into balance and alignment. Therefore, for the wheels to remain in equilibrium, they must all turn at the same time. The elements of love, compassion, and joy are all represented by the fourth chakra. It's one of the most stunning, but also emotionally charged, chakras that individuals can use. Love, compassion, forgiveness, and acceptance of others (as well as yourself) are all present when this chakra is balanced. Codependence, high or low blood pressure, manipulative behaviors, and feelings of worthlessness can all occur when you're out of harmony.

The corresponding hue is green. By immediately enhancing the fourth chakra's beneficial traits, you can directly open it. Keep a thankfulness notebook, for instance, in which you list three things for which you are grateful each day. Alternately, engage in metta meditation, which encourages compassion for all living things.

Location: Center of the Chest

Element: Air

Color: Green

Meaning: Compassion and Love

Symbol Components

Twelve-Petalled Lotus: The heart chakra's twelve petals stand for the twelve heavenly attributes related to the heart: harmony, serenity, bliss, love, pureness, clarity, compassion, unity, forgiveness, and kindness.

Hexagram: The hexagram is symbolized by two triangles, one looking upward and the other downward, to form a six-pointed star symbolizing the intertwining of male and female energies.

Throat (Visshudha Chakra)

The first of the three spiritual chakras is the Visshudha, often known as the throat chakra. It is the fifth wheel of energy. Ether, an element that represents open speech from which honesty and integrity can flow, is connected to the throat chakra. The fifth chakra stands for your capacity to communicate clearly, tell your truth, and be aware of both your inner and exterior intentions. The lower four chakras must be in harmony with it because it is the first of the spiritual chakras. When this chakra is in harmony, you communicate and express yourself with a higher level of authenticity. An out-of-alignment throat chakra can cause a sore throat, thyroid issues, neck/shoulder pain, and difficulty speaking your truth or asking for what you need, want, or desire. Light blue is the corresponding hue. Singing, chanting, shouting out loud affirmations, or practicing public speaking will strengthen the life force of this chakra.

Location: Throat

Element: Ether

Color: Blue

Meaning: Communication

Symbol Components

The sixteen-petalled lotus of the throat chakra is a comparison to the sixteen Sanskrit vowels. In turn, the light and simple pronunciation of those vowels represent the airy nature of communication. This is why communication skills are impacted by a blocked throat chakra.

The inverted triangle: A direct expression of our higher self, the inverted triangle represents a channel to our consciousness and soul body.

A circle lying inside of a triangle, which stands for the full moon, indicates the throat chakra. This represents a cleansed mind.

Third Eye (Ajna Chakra)

The third eye chakra, which represents our sixth sense or intuition, is the sixth energy wheel. Its position in the space between the brows is crucial to how we live, how we view the outside world, and how we communicate with ourselves. When this chakra is in complete balance, you can make decisions and confront obstacles in life with confidence, the ego fades into the background, and you may start to figure out what you genuinely value in life. When out of alignment, you may be cynical, overly logical, and untrusting, and you may experience eyesight, headache, and migraine problems. Indigo is the corresponding hue. The third eye can be opened up by practices like meditation that calm the mind and slow the mental process. Practices like visualization and manifestation, in particular, pique your imagination and draw on this center's virtues.

Location: Between the Eyes

Element: Light

Color: Indigo

Meaning: Imagination

Symbol Components

Two-Petalled Lotus: The third eye chakra's two petals represent the idea of a dualistic relationship between the Self and God.

The inverted triangle stands for your relationship with the divine and genuine enlightenment.

Crown (Sahasrara Chakra)

The seventh and last chakra is the Sahasrara, or crown chakra. It stands in for our spiritual selves. This chakra symbolizes your divine nature, which is enjoying a human experience on Earth. By focusing on this chakra, you let the world and yourself know that you are prepared to let go of boundaries, merge with everything, and leave the material realm for something more spiritual. A source of enlightenment, spiritual connection, and connection to our higher self is present when this chakra is in balance. When you're out of harmony, you think that happiness comes from the outside, but it actually originates from within. On the other hand, you can be overly sensitive to your divine nature and find it difficult to carry out your regular daily duties. The corresponding hue is purple (violet). You can widen the seventh chakra and strengthen your connection to the cosmos by meditating and engaging in other spiritual activities. Reading spiritual writings and novels can increase spiritual awareness, and stargazing can help you feel connected to the universe.

While working with this energy, you start expressing your interest in some higher purpose and an enlightened way of being when you deal with this energy point. The crown chakra serves as a portal to super-consciousness, a condition of existence in which it is impossible to perceive oneself as distinct from anything or anybody.

Location: Top of the Head

Element: None

Color: Violet or Purple

Meaning: Intelligence and Awareness

Symbol Components

Lotus with a Thousand Petals: The thousand petals stand for a person's relationship to the divine and our shared humanity with the universe. The lotus flower represents the wealth and enduring nature of these vital ties.

The full moon is symbolized by the circle, a representation of openness and a conscious mind awakening.

THE TWELVE CHAKRAS SYSTEM

In addition to the above basic seven energy centers, several yogis thought there might be many more. For instance, they believed that those seven chakras are linked to 72,000 nadis (energy streams) and 114 sub-chakras in the human physical body. The chakras can be divided into 21 minor chakras, 86 micro-chakras, and 7 major chakras. The spine is home to the seven primary chakras. The remainder, however, are dispersed across body parts like the feet or knees or situated outside of the actual body. Besides the basic seven chakras, experts have identified six more definitive energy centers inside and outside of the body. Since those energy centers also affect our aura, they are also now included in chakra healing therapy. The presence of the twelve-chakra system is one of the most recent ideas held by new-age believers. The seven major chakras and an additional five (or six) outer chakras are included in this transpersonal and sub-personal system. These new chakras are extracorporeal and symbolize our connection to higher spiritual planes. Each chakra has a distinct function and possesses unique traits that have an impact on a certain area of our mind, body, or soul. According to the twelve-chakra system, other than the basic seven chakras—root, sacral, solar plexus, throat, heart, third eye, and crown—there are five more chakras, named soul star, spirit star, universal, galactic, and divine gateway. There is yet another chakra, the "earth star chakra," which is marked as zero on this list due to its positioning; it is present below the feet and above the ground. Here is what the rest of the chakras represent:

Earth Star Chakra

Vasundhara, or the earth star chakra, is a "sub-personal" chakra situated beneath the feet. Although the exact location of the energy center is uncertain, it is thought to be between six and eighteen inches below the soles of your feet. The earth star chakra is known as the "grounding thread" that draws our "light body" to the heart of the earth and possesses a grounding, earthy energy similar to the root chakra. When not activated, the corresponding color is black, and when it is, it is magenta (purplish red).

The earth star and the root chakra both share many of the same characteristics, allowing you to feel grounded and centered and work effectively on the physical level as a result. This includes the capacity to keep a job, manage finances, and take care of your health through exercise and a healthy diet. In contrast, if this chakra is inactive, a person may live a self-destructive life, battle addictions, and have a difficult time maintaining order. In today's world, the earth star chakra enables you to slow down and get in touch with nature to prevent burnout from a fast-paced lifestyle. It can assist us in maintaining equilibrium and staying centered.

Walking barefoot on the ground is one efficient approach to opening the earth star' chakra. One of the best ways to really strengthen the earth element within us is through this. You can perform this activity anyplace; however, natural ground like grass or sand is preferable over concrete pavements for comfort. Keep your mind on the present moment when "earthing" and concentrate on the sensation of the ground under your feet because, like with all chakra healing treatments, conscious attention is crucial.

How do we harmonize our earth star chakras? Actually, it's quite simple. Get outside, for starters! A great way to start is by getting in touch with the earth. After all, in order to connect with something, you need to be familiar with it! You might feel more connected by making judgments that consider the earth and the planet. I suggest you give it a try if you practically never camp, hike the outdoors, or go barefoot outside.

Moreover, meditation is an effective method for balancing the chakras. In particular, a "tree meditation" may be helpful because it can help you picture your roots extending all the way deep to the earth's core, which will center your earth star chakra once more. It's also crucial to understand that no chakra, not even the earth star, can resolve all problems by itself. The seven primary chakras in the body, as well as other chakras like the earth star chakra, all need nurturing.

Soul Star Chakra

The eighth energy center, known as the soul star chakra or Sitara in Sanskrit, is situated six to twelve inches above the seventh chakra. The eighth chakra, which symbolizes a brilliant circle of heavenly light over your head, is also known as the halo chakra. This transpersonal chakra is situated above the physical body and stands in for the upper etheric levels. It acts as the main pathway for divine energy to flow to the other chakras below. Its corresponding hue is fern green. Past lifetimes and karmic cycles are also connected to this energy area. You can use it to access the Akashic records, an energetic repository for information that contains specifics of your soul's journey. It enables you to nurture peace and discover your life's purpose in the current world. The most effective methods for directing the energy of the soul star are spiritual exercises like yoga and meditation. Visualization is particularly powerful. Visualize radiant light flowing through your seven main chakras, connecting to the etheric body as it descends from the sky. Imagine the light purifying your soul and revealing your mission before leaving you whole, both physically and spiritually. Moreover, as this chakra is associated with the process of letting go, letting go of unfavorable thinking patterns and behaviors might aid in activating it.

Universal Chakra

The tenth chakra, situated above the spirit chakra, is known as the universal chakra. It represents the color pearl white and controls all facets of existence. Here, our masculine and feminine energies come together, enabling us to access the best aspects of both. The entrance to the illimitable river of creation is the universe chakra. When activated, your "light being" and physical existence are perfectly in tune with the universe.

Galactic Chakra

Time travel is associated with the eleventh chakra, also known as the galactic chakra, which also possesses supernatural abilities like teleportation, quick manifestation, and bilocation. When this energy center is active, a person may transcend the boundaries of time and space and embrace all cosmic understanding. It is thought that the galactic chakra is either pink-orange or a blend of violet, gold, and silver. A light-language vocal activation meditation can help you connect to the energy of the galactic chakra. Chant the mantra "*Cha Numi Go Loa Sho*" while picturing a diamond crystal, like in this guided meditation.

Stellar Chakra

This chakra stands for the vast spiritual realm and connecting with angels, light beings, and guides. The hue that goes with it is turquoise (blue green). While activating your spirit chakra gives you access to all of your soul's talents and powers and opening your soul star chakra helps you discover your real purpose, this direct connection to the divine boosts your capacity to manifest and create.

Since the words "star" and "space" are derived from each other, the chakra is known as the "portal to the stellar." In order to save humans from being overwhelmed by energy and universal truths, the Stellar Gateway was created. Human minds are not able to assimilate higher frequencies easily as we would want. We must go through phases of gradually boosting our frequency in order to understand, process, and handle information and experiences at higher frequencies. Our bodies and minds could not handle the energy if we were able to access all of the universal truths, which might be to our detriment.

Divine Gateway Chakra

The divine gateway chakra, also referred to as the stellar entrance chakra, is the last of the twelve chakras. The culmination of the chakra path symbolizes total ascension and union with the divine. The entrance to the divine world is opened by turning on this energy. A person who has awakened this chakra is said to possess the spiritual wisdom to help others on their chakra journeys toward cosmic connection. The twelfth chakra appears as shimmering energy that is golden or multicolored.

WHY BALANCE YOUR CHAKRAS?

Our physical bodies and energy centers dwell in different worlds. Our mind, which is the very tip of our consciousness, tries to make these bodily areas more conscious. Consider your physical characteristics. Your physical body begins to manufacture antibodies and red blood cells to treat you when you catch a cold or a cut on your finger. However, because your soul dwells in the physical world, your physical body is unable to do that for it. The energy centers are located in the psychospiritual plane of existence, also referred to as the subtle body. How, then, can we address imbalances and motivate our energy healer to start healing?

We can have a chamomile tea yearning or feel the need to take off our shoes and go barefoot. These intuitive actions assist us in rebalancing and realigning. In terms of the human experience, ego is more audible than intuition. The influence of outside stimuli can muddle the mind. In order to align our chakras and unblock our energy centers, we must work purposefully at it. Without our physical bodies automatically taking care of it for us, we must put extra effort and practice into taking care of our chakras. What happens when we are conscious of the necessity for chakra balance? What takes place when we deliberately realign our energy centers? Here are several reasons to practice chakra alignment.

To be grounded. Your lack of feeling grounded causes you to seek outside validation, and you feel uncertain about your life's course. Distrusting our inner guidance can usually put us in dubious, if not worse, energy-draining circumstances. As a result, we get distracted from our intended course. With loads of sorrow, pain, and uncertainty in tow, it begins to resemble a slackline being walked by a want-to-be trapeze performer. However, when we align ourselves and unblock the root chakra, we feel nourished from the inside rather than the outside. When you declare, "I am anchored, I am strong," it is much harder to knock you off balance.

To follow your life's calling. Have you ever had a sense of being cut off from yourself? Are you a passenger in this rundown car, not the driver, and do you have no idea where you're going? It is not shameful to not know who or where you are supposed to be. The identity we project to the outside world is usually influenced by our physical bodies. We cannot pick our parents, the country in which we are born, or even the physical characteristics of our body. When we begin to identify ourselves with something that we are not, our solar plexus chakra becomes out of alignment. Be mindful of how you communicate with yourself. Do you treat yourself well? When you start to hear yourself saying things like:

- Why do you lack her intelligence?
- You're not as prosperous as they are.
- Why don't I know what I want to accomplish with my life yet?
- What's the matter with me?

These are signals that your spiritual alignment needs some care.

To align your inner and outer worlds. Our planet is kept alive and humming with vigor by nature. It only seems natural that the color green would be connected to the heart chakra in our inner self. Our heart is what keeps us active, compassionate, alive, and healthy, just like nature. We are more open to the energy of the universe when our inner and outer worlds are in harmony. This energy can readily flow through us if our chakra systems are unobstructed. As a result, we develop into healthier humans. Mental or physical illnesses cannot destabilize us. When our chakra energy center is stable, we receive nourishment not from the outside in but rather from the inside out.

To create your own reality. Sometimes in life, we put obstacles in our path. We put a block within ourselves when we avoid talking about things that upset us out of fear of being judged, when we are not open about what we desire, and when we are afraid of being judged. As a result, we stifle our development, set boundaries on our options, and jeopardize our happiness. The magic of being able to talk without inhibition exists. Our voices are a potent force for influencing the world around us. So always speak the truth and do it with love. Only discuss topics about which you have knowledge and are aware of as being true.

Use your physical vision to guide your decisions. When something doesn't turn out to your best advantage, have you ever found yourself exclaiming, "I knew this was going to happen"? That typically occurs because your intuition alerts you, but you choose not to heed it. How would it feel to live a life where you always made the right decisions for yourself? Stop the things that do not benefit you from happening instead of just stating, "Well, I knew this was going to happen."

When we don't believe in ourselves or ignore that inner voice, our third eye chakra becomes blocked. Moreover, our intuition is always accurate. That inner voice is always aware of your best interests. Instead of relying on retrospection, let your intuition be your guide to access the ability of foresight.

To establish a connection with your spirituality and higher self. All we have to do to allow the universe's river of energy to flow to and through us is to be open to receiving it. Connecting with the infinite source of energy means connecting with all that is present in the cosmos. The ultimate definition of the path of least resistance is having our whole self—mind, body, and spirit—aligned. You can start to feel love, joy, and clarity again in your life once you start going with that flow. It is a condition of overall well-being and tranquility. When we are in balance, we are operating at our best.

We may endure miseries, including mental and physical ailments, when a chakra is out of balance. Our feeling of having to struggle more can result from this misery spreading to other aspects of our lives. Our consciousness is dispersed throughout this seven-chakra system. We feel a condition of harmony and calm when our chakras are open and in alignment. When you are at your best, it naturally affects how you interact with other people and the outside environment. You are connected to everything, confident in your mission, and truthful with both yourself and others.

BOOK 2:
YOGA AND MEDITATION

Have you ever practically tried yoga and meditation yourself? If you haven't, then read on! This book has everything you need to know about those practices. When it comes to spiritual and chakra healing, meditation and yoga are the two most highly recommended therapeutic methods. It's not just the chakras that they unlock, but by regularly doing yoga and meditation, you can connect to your inner strength. There is a special connection between these methods and the energy that flows through us. And if you want to find out all about it, then I have a complete guide on meditation, its types, the poses, and ways to get started right here in this book. Besides that, all the yoga practices, their importance, and the poses for yoga for each chakra are also discussed. After a thorough reading of the different parts of this book, you will feel more equipped and enthused about practicing meditation and yoga in your daily routine.

CHAKRA AND MEDITATION CONNECTION

Any style of meditation that aims to unblock chakras and tap into the strength of these energy centers throughout the body is referred to as chakra meditation. It can be employed for a variety of purposes, including fostering serenity, relaxation, and spiritual awakening. Basically, a self-monitored exercise should be sufficient if your goal is to feel more balanced or calm or even just to have an easier time falling asleep. Your greatest option, if you have more serious goals, is to take advice from the experts. The types of self-guided chakra meditations you can do at home usually aim to foster a sense of contentment, calm, and stronger identity. Whatever style of chakra meditation you choose to practice, the ultimate objective is to have fully opened chakras that allow energy to freely flow throughout your body and foster a strong connection between your mind and body.

Many other methods have been used to characterize the goal of yogic disciplines, including the realization of the self, the finding of truth, and the realization of one's own identity. Yoga has two meanings in Sanskrit. The initial meaning, "union," here denotes stability, harmony, and unity. The second meaning, "yoke," like the device used to connect oxen pulling a wagon, denotes the fusion of the human ego with the divine. This union can be achieved by focusing on an inner true self or other sacred symbol or entity, such as a chakra, mandala, or mantra. The achievement of this objective requires the total negation of the discrete, separate self, which stands in the way of the seeker's pursuit of unrestricted freedom. The aspirant can only start living at a higher level when the negation of individuality is realized, where everything, including the individual self, is encompassed as one.

True life is born from this union, and it is this union that opens the door to spiritual emancipation. Self-negation and self-realization are not in any way incompatible when viewed in this light. Union with God, the ultimate aim of yoga, can finally be attained as one raises the degree of existence via sustained practice. This is unlike our everyday perspective, in which subject and object exist as separate, independent entities. In fact, the separation between subject and object is the foundation of science. A scientist tries to carefully investigate phenomena and develop theories that account for what he has seen. However, the observer himself is not considered; as a result, the knowledge acquired is knowledge about the item alone, not the subject who has identified and perceived the object. In this way, science is incomplete since it does not study the entire area of observation.

Contrarily, knowledge gained through the integration of subject and object considers both parties' reality as well as the underlying unity of the universe from which they originate. This combination of subject and object is what is known as a key objective of the yogic practice of samadhi. In scientific practice, the five sensory organs are used as a filter to perceive an object. However, in yogic practice, when an issue is brought up, a thing rejected, something is opposed, or something is in opposition to the object's fundamental essence, it might transcend the five sensory filters and be directed by the superconscious, as opposed to through means of the sense organs. We can refer to this way of understanding as wisdom. Yoga aims to achieve the state of subject and object unity that is the home of true wisdom. Chakra activation is a crucial tool for achieving this objective. The best approach to gain "siddhis" is through tantric yoga's chakra awakening procedures, which improve both physical and mental capabilities.

Benefits of Chakra Meditation

So how does one go about practicing a chakra meditation? It actually depends on the person because meditation evolves with each sitting. I advise using the hues related to each chakra as a focal point if you're a visual person. Others find it simpler to put a hand on each spot to express how they feel and to direct attention there while leading themselves through the meditation.

Remember that meditation does not absolutely require closed eyelids; it may be done with open eyes as a way to focus and soften the mind but consider candle meditation as an example. During the entire practice, you sit with your eyes wide open, gazing at the flame. You may thus have a visual cue of the chakra points in front of you and, as you concentrate on each point, align them with the corresponding place on your own body, progressing from the root to the crown. I'd suggest acquiescing once you've reached the crown and closing your eyes. If you prefer audio, guided chakra meditations are wonderful since they usually specify not only the name of each chakra but also its location and color, allowing you to use visualization as you progress through the meditation.

IDENTIFYING CHAKRAS TO HEAL

Have you recently felt "off"? Are you making silly mistakes at work? Have you been ill for three weeks running? These upsetting conditions could be caused by several factors, but they could also be a symptom of a chakra system imbalance. How do chakras work? And what are the symptoms of an unbalanced chakra system? The body has energy centers called chakras. Despite the fact that there are numerous chakras, seven major ones are usually the focus of attention. These bright energy wheels are aligned along the Sushumna nadi, the body's main conduit.

The power centers where the left energy channel (Ida nadi) and the right energy channel (Pingala nadi) connect are the chakras along the Sushumna nadi. What is termed as "the subtle body" is composed of these energy pathways and psycho-power centers. The mind and physical body are in different realms, but the subtle body has a significant influence on all three. When the nadis and chakras are open and prana can flow easily throughout the system, the human body system thrives. Harmony is the aim. Blockage and imbalance can result from any type of disorder or illness in the body, mind, or spirit. So, if you've been feeling off, examine your chakras more closely to figure out what's going on and start to find balance and harmony.

Think about what you have been consuming (food, drink, thoughts, experiences), your present life circumstances (traveling, moving, major changes), and the ongoing season if you are feeling out of balance (wind, cold, rain, heat, dryness). Each of these elements has the ability to have a significant impact on your entire delicate human system. Understanding your chakras is crucial to comprehending the human system in the philosophy of yoga and Ayurveda, where "like increases like" and "opposites balance." This means that if your body already has an excess amount of heat (such as rage or indigestion) and you add more heat (such as spicy food), you may feel even hotter, agitated, and more frustrated. You might feel better and be more in balance, though, if you add the reverse to that equation and take a cold relaxing shower or eat some juicy, fresh fruit.

Are Your Chakras Balanced?

There are generally five indicators that your chakras may not be in balance. Too much or too little energy in any of the chakras, when trying to achieve equilibrium, leads to imbalance. Keep in mind that harmony is the ultimate aim; chakra balancing requires effort. The typical red flags are:

- You feel "off" in reaction to something.
- You become ill.
- You become ill, again.
- You start making careless errors.
- Everything seems to be breaking down.

Specific emotional, physical, mental, and spiritual imbalances in each chakra result from each of these general imbalances. Let's examine more closely how this might contribute to a feeling of disharmony throughout the body system.

Signs of Blocked Root Chakra

The root chakra is connected with the element of earth and is physically placed at the feet, legs, and "roots" of your being. The root chakra is directly connected to the sense of security and comfort in your own flesh. The human tribe and your family of origin are likewise connected to this chakra. You may have a root chakra imbalance if you experience any of the following signs:

- Stiffness and discomfort in your legs and feet
- Excessive hamstring flexibility or a lack of physical stability
- A lack of security and safety
- Feeling erratic and unsettled at home
- A perception of being trapped in life or a lack of flexibility

To bring into balance:

- Hike, walk in the sand, or plant a garden to get in touch with the environment.
- Eat fruit and vegetables—food that comes from the land.
- Practice grounding breathing techniques like alternate nostril breathing and sama vritti.
- Put on something red.
- Move your legs with stretches and exercises.

Connecting to the soil is a rapid approach to balancing the root chakra. To root is the key to your root chakra. Do you feel balanced, anchored, safe, centered, and earthed? To balance my root chakra, I prefer to put my bare feet on the ground and feel myself grounding down. I enjoy meditating on the earth's grounding energy while directing my attention to my feet, which serve as an anchor for my secure and stable body.

Signs of Blocked Sacral Chakra

This sacred chakra is connected to the element of water and is physically placed at the sacrum, hips, and sexual organs. Feelings, imagination, and sensations are connected to your sacral chakra. Moreover, this chakra is your connection to intimacy and one-on-one relationships. You may have a blockage in the sacral chakra if you experience any of the conditions listed below:

- Hip and low back pain and stiffness
- Being easily emotionally drained
- Loss of creativity and imagination
- Walled off and lacking in emotional sensitivity
- Reproductive and sexual issues

To restore balance:

- Drink water, go swimming, or take a relaxing bath to connect with the element of water.
- Dance.
- Use journaling or counseling to connect with your emotions.
- Put on something orange.
- Stretch and move your hips.

Signs of Blocked Solar Plexus Chakra

The solar plexus chakra is connected with the element of fire and physically placed at the midback, side, and belly. The solar plexus chakra is linked to all of your self-perceived thoughts and emotions. This chakra is concerned with how you relate to yourself. This chakra is out of balance if you experience any of the symptoms listed below:

- Digestive problems and tummy aches
- A low sense of self
- Bloated ego, lack of commitment
- Inability to complete tasks on time

To restore balance:

- Consider meditating on a candle flame or bonfire to connect with the element of fire.
- Consume easy-to-digest foods.
- Go outside and enjoy the sun.
- Put on something yellow.
- Improve your core stability and learn detoxifying twists.

Signs of Blocked Heart Chakra

Physically located in the heart, arms, hands, chest, shoulders, and upper back, this chakra is linked to the element of air. All types of love, including self-love, friendship, family love, romantic love, and empathy for others, are associated with the heart chakra. You might have an imbalance in the heart chakra if you experience any of the following signs:

- Upper back or chest pain
- Tight shoulders or shoulders that are too flexible
- Inability to accept love in any of its manifestations
- Lack of compassion for oneself
- Having a lack of or sense of loss in terms of love

To restore balance:

- Breathe deeply and go outside to connect with the element of air.
- For yourself and others, practice loving-kindness/Metta meditation.
- Take care of yourself, love yourself, and spread love.
- Put on some green or pink clothing.
- Extend your hands, arms, hands, shoulders, upper back, and chest.

Signs of Blocked Throat Chakra

Physically located in the throat, neck, mouth, jaw, and ears, this chakra is linked to the element of ether/space. The throat chakra is connected to expression, using your voice, and knowing when to be quiet. This chakra is linked to your ability to communicate clearly from the heart and mind while listening compassionately. You might have an imbalance in the throat chakra if you experience any of the following signs.:

- Throat infection or laryngitis
- Jaw discomfort or a history of teeth grinding
- Having neck discomfort or stiffness
- A tendency to chatter constantly or an inability to know when to be quiet
- Inability to assert oneself, create boundaries or defend oneself

To restore balance

- Chant the mantra or sing it.
- Enjoy calming tea or water with lemon.
- Become a silent meditator.
- Put on some turquoise clothing.
- Listen to lovely music.

Signs of Blocked Third Eye Chakra

This chakra is physically located inside the mind, between the eyebrows, and in the middle of your forehead. Your inner creativity, understanding, and intelligence are connected to your third eye chakra. This chakra is also connected to your capacity to look deeply within your heart areas to your most authentic, wisest selves. You can see the wider picture and have a positive outlook on the future when the third eye chakra is open. You might have a third eye chakra imbalance if you experience any of these signs:

- Headaches
- Mental haze
- Absence of intuitive direction
- Not feeling inspired
- Excessively active imagination

To restore balance

- Pay attention to and respect the signals that your body sends you.
- Maintain a dream notebook.
- Put on something blue.
- Work on balancing poses like Dancer's Pose and Tree Pose.
- Yoga poses should be done with closed eyes.

Signs of Blocked the Crown Chakra

The top of the head and skull are where this chakra is situated physically. Your sense of enlightenment and the knowledge that you are a small component of a larger whole are linked to your head chakra. The sense of where you fit in the universe is also connected to this chakra. You might have an imbalance in the head chakra if you experience any of the symptoms listed below:

- Headaches
- inability to focus or pay proper attention to the current task
- Drama in your life that seems to be ongoing
- Inability to look beyond your own space
- Lack of ability to empathize with others or adopt their opinions

To restore balance

- Put meditation to use.
- Participate in volunteer activities.
- Keep an appreciation notebook.
- Put on something purple.
- Practice inverted yoga poses such as a headstand.

UNDERSTANDING MEDITATION

Meditation is a type of mental practice that teaches you to maintain your attention on a single idea, objective, or experience, like your breath. The goal of meditation is to quiet racing thoughts. Regular practice can aid consciousness transformation in a way that encourages inner tranquility, mental clarity, emotional positivity, profound knowing, and focus, as well as allow us to find our feet when we feel dispersed. The mind can cease straying and become engrossed in thoughts, emotions, or other mental distractions by keeping focused attention, such as the breath, a mantra, or another tool. Visualizations, in which you develop a mental picture geared toward a certain goal, can also be a part of meditation. You can enhance your connection with each chakra by visualizing its colors or energy flow. You can learn to moderate your reactions to stimuli that may otherwise generate painful or disturbing reactions because meditation requires the capacity to observe diverting thoughts and feelings without judgment. The ability to be mindful can be a very effective technique for developing peace and compassion in daily life. It can also be a means of strengthening and establishing a connection with your chakras. Meditation can help you connect more deeply with your physical and energy bodies by allowing you to become aware of what you are holding in a specific energy center.

There are many different ways to try meditation, including sitting or lying down, remaining still, or doing something else, like walking, making art, listening to music, or keeping a journal. While some people meditate for only 5 to 10 minutes each day, others may do so for longer.

Types of Meditation

A discipline that has stood the test of time is meditation. It has experienced a resurgence in popularity in the last few years, probably due to the fact that many of us desire to build a practice to calm our minds and bring tranquility to our hectic lives! But it's more than just a trend. In fact, a 2016 study published in Consciousness and Cognition indicated that both experienced and inexperienced meditators experience a reduction in the physiological signs of anger after just one session of meditation. On the plus side, meditation can be practiced at any time, any place, and for any length of time. It strengthens our sense of self and facilitates our transition into greater consciousness. Moreover, it enables us to access our ability for mindfulness and self-healing, which spreads tranquility throughout the rest of our life. Moreover, meditation complements any self-study routine you may currently have because it grows on itself.

Visualization Meditation

In order to focus and center the mind and body during meditation, visualization involves focusing on an image or series of images in mind. Any relaxing image that brings you serenity can be effective; however, there are frequently several images that are widely used that may be helpful. There are seven primary methods of visualization meditation. They can be divided into two categories. Techniques that urge us to view with our mind's eyes and those that emphasize picturing something concrete outside of the body. Think about one or more of these meditation practices to develop a visualization routine that suits you.

Yantra or mandala. Contemplating a yantra, which is usually done in tantric rituals, can be an effective way to concentrate awareness. Any mandala, though, can be used as a meditation tool even if it has no particular purpose. With our eyes open or internalized, we can create new neural connections in the brain by imagining symmetrical and repeated patterns, which promotes feelings of harmony, clarity, and calm.

Guru or deity. Visualizing a spiritual teacher or a god and calling on its attributes is central to many spiritual traditions. Keep in mind that gods and goddesses reflect many attributes of the divine and of ourselves in both Buddhism and Hinduism. Finding a deity that you can relate to and whose characteristics you want to embody in your life is a good place to start because when we see deities, we concentrate on doing the same in our own lives.

Anything else you feel is important. If none of the aforementioned items catch your attention, try imagining a candle flame, a flower, the sun, the moon, your favorite location, or the face or eyes of a loved one. Any object that makes you feel calm or at peace can aid in your journey toward greater self-awareness and serves as an appropriate emblem for visualization.

Energy or chakra. Concentrating on light or energy within your body is a frequent internal visualization exercise. One approach to do this is to concentrate on either a particular chakra (such as the third eye, heart, etc.) or on each chakra in turn as a spectrum of light and color. These energy centers can be visualized as lights, flames, lotus flowers, or dense areas of spinning energy if you are unable to discern color.

Creative journeys that are guided. Journey-style visualization, which is typically scripted, can be helpful for people who have problems focusing their minds or who are looking for insight into daily life. These meditations typically start with a relaxation technique and then involve a walk outdoors with symbolic objects or roadblocks that you might come across along the way. Usually, the purpose of these techniques is to help you communicate with various areas of your subconscious mind.

It can also be powerful to take charge of your own trip, particularly one that takes you through a trying circumstance in life so that you can see yourself making decisions that will benefit you. Various theories propose the idea that our ideas affect our realities; therefore, imagining real-life events can serve as a powerful exercise in conquering problems and generating the behaviors that you want to realize.

Color breathing. Select a trait or feeling that you wish to have more of in your life by giving it some thought. Next, choose a hue that most closely represents this quality or feeling. For instance, you might select a calming blue or an invigorating orange if you want to feel happy. Green may be your best option if you wish to feel peaceful. When you're prepared, close your eyes, and take several deep breaths. Consider the hue you choose and picture it in your head. Feel the color cover your face, legs, feet, arms, chest, hands, and fingers as you inhale. Take a deep breath in, then allow the color to flood your entire body. You can breathe out and keep your attention on the color, or you can feel as though you are breathing out any unfavorable emotions.

Mindfulness Meditation

Mindfulness meditation is the practice of being completely present. Being mindful involves being aware of our behaviors and our environment, as well as avoiding overreacting to them. Anywhere is suitable for attentive meditation. Sitting quietly, keeping their eyes closed, and focusing solely on their breathing might be more calming for some people. But you may make the decision to be mindful at any time of the day, even while you're performing your chores or driving to work. When practicing mindfulness meditation, you become aware of your thoughts and feelings yet allow them to pass without getting upset.

You can practice mindfulness meditation in practically any place. Bring your attention to the physical breath and body sensations, such as the rising and falling of the chest and abdomen or the sensation of the breath as it enters and exits the mouth or nose. You could also concentrate on any nearby sounds or odors. When you are comfortable, bring your awareness to your thoughts and feelings, allowing them to enter and then leave. Think of your thoughts as ever-changing clouds drifting across a bright blue sky.

Transcendental Meditation

Despite its lofty sound, transcendental meditation is a straightforward technique: You select a mantra, such as a word, phrase, or sound, and repeat it twice daily for 20 minutes. It is recommended to perform this while seated and with closed eyes. By meditating in this way, you can completely unwind your body and mind and experience serenity and quiet. Find a certified Transcendental Meditation teacher who can give you a mantra to start the meditation process. This mantra is determined by a wide range of variables, including the practitioner's birth year and the teacher's training year. Spend 20 minutes twice a day sitting and reciting this phrase.

Guided Meditation

Guided meditation, also known as guided imagery or visualization, is a type of meditation practice in which you create relaxing mental images or scenarios in your head. "Guided" refers to the fact that this process is usually led by a teacher or guide. It's frequently advised to induce calmness in your relaxing place by appealing to as many senses as you can, including fragrance, sounds, and textures. Finding a teacher you enjoy and connect with is key in this situation. Additionally, you can limit your search to a particular outcome and test out guided meditations that are geared toward acceptance, stress reduction, or sleep.

Vipassana Meditation

The phrase "seeing things for what they are" is the translation of the traditional Indian meditation practice known as vipassana. It has been practiced for over 2,500 years and is credited with inspiring the US to adopt the practice of mindfulness meditation. Vipassana meditation uses introspection to try to change the person. By focusing on the physical sensations in your body, you can establish a solid connection between your mind and body. This interconnectivity, according to the practice's teachers, promotes love and compassion while aiding in mind balance. A 10-day course is frequently used to teach vipassana, during which time pupils are expected to refrain from things like alcohol and sexual activity.

Focus on the breath as it flows through the body while taking a peaceful seat. Allow all feelings, sensations, ideas, and sounds to come without attaching yourself to them. Label any interruptions—for instance, "a bird chirping"—and then shift your attention back to your breathing.

Metta Meditation

Practicing loving-kindness meditation, commonly referred to as metta meditation, involves concentrating positive thoughts on other people. The words and phrases that practitioners speak are meant to inspire benevolence. This is frequently seen in mindfulness and Vipassana meditation as well. It is typically carried out while slouching comfortably.

Inhale a few times deeply before repeating the sentences slowly and evenly. These include: "I hope to be happy. I wish you well. I'm hoping I'm okay. I long for comfort and peace." When you have practiced this loving kindness for yourself for some time, you may begin to think of a family member or acquaintance who has been helpful to you and repeat the mantra again, this time changing "I" to "you."

Find a comfortable position and, while keeping your eyes closed, focus your attention on the middle of your heart on your chest. Imagine that when you inhale, you are taking in warmth, compassion, and unwavering love for yourself. As you exhale, visualize that you are sending that same warmth, compassion, and unwavering love outward to the people around you. Start with close friends or family members, then direct it toward neutral acquaintances, people you don't particularly like right now, and finally, strangers. Practitioners are also urged to picture clients with whom they have trouble working. You finish the meditation by repeating the phrase, "May all beings everywhere be happy."

Chakra Meditation

The word "chakra," which means "wheel" in ancient Sanskrit, has its roots in India. Chakras are the term used to describe the energy and spiritual power centers in the human body. There are thought to be seven chakras. Each chakra is located at a specific spot along the body's spine and has a corresponding color. Through the use of relaxation techniques, chakra meditation aims to bring balance and well-being to the chakras. One of these methods is to visualize each chakra in the body together with its corresponding color. Some folks may decide to light incense or use gems that match each chakra's color to help them focus while meditating.

Yoga Meditation

In India, yoga has been practiced since the Stone Age. Despite the wide range of yoga classes and styles, all involve practicing a series of postures and controlled breathing techniques intended to improve flexibility and calm the mind. It depends on a number of factors, like the kind of meditation you choose to do. Because the postures require balance and concentration, practitioners are taught to ignore distractions and stay. Talk to your doctor about which yoga style could be great for you if you are new to yoga and have a health concern.

Keep your focus on your present-moment physical feelings and breathing while performing any yoga pose. Every time you notice your attention straying to other ideas, gently bring it back. One of the best routes for meditation is corpse posture (Savasana), which is done at the conclusion of every yoga class.

Yin And Yang Meditation

Yin and yang meditation is a good choice for when you're depressed, unmotivated, or energetically detached. First, give yourself a few moments to collect yourself. Find a comfortable, upright sitting position and equally distribute your weight among your sitting bones, so your head feels as though it is resting on top of your spine. Close your eyes first, then focus on your breathing. Inhale gently for four counts, followed by a leisurely six-count exhalation. Repeat this several times until you feel like your breath has stabilized. Then resume regular, gentle breathing. Imagine yourself being anchored to Mother Earth by thick roots that grow from your feet and extend forth into the dirt, rock, and sand. Imagine that these roots are carrying goodness, love, and nourishment from the earth all the way up to your heart, which is located just below your navel.

Visualize a golden thread coming out of the top of your head, climbing to the sky, holding you up, and connecting you to the brilliant, vast energy of the sky. The sun's warm, golden light enters your body through your head and gradually moves down your body to the region just below your naval, where it combines with the energy of the ground.

The two energies support and nourish you because you are a part of them, and they are a part of you. You carry the strength and vigor of the ground and the sky because of your connection to both. You are present, capable, and flexible. You have the energy that was passed down to you from your parents, their parents, and all of your ancestors since the dawn of time. They are all gathered close to you, supporting you with their vigor. Spend some time meditating and becoming aware of your inner energies. Consider how everything is connected to you and how you are the center of the universe's natural equilibrium.

GETTING STARTED WITH MEDITATION

Everyone can benefit from the simple practice of meditation, which can lower stress, improve relaxation and clarity, and foster happiness. The benefits of meditation can start to manifest right away and learning how to do it is simple. Here, we provide some fundamental advice to get you started on the road to more composure, acceptance, and joy. Inhale deeply, then prepare to unwind. When practicing chakra meditation, you are actively involved with your entire body, exploring its layers on a healing level, and experiencing the effects of ideas and feelings. It's a very individualized practice, but I would say you may anticipate feelings of fulfillment, tranquility, and heightened energy. You ought to get more rest and feel more connected to who you are. Consider your chakras as a toolbox. To use your tools to their full potential, you must keep them well-kept and sharp. Working on these ideas on a regular basis will enable you to rapidly access the best tool when bad or negative things happen in life. Here is how you can prepare yourself well for a daily dose of meditation:

Make your space ready. Setting up your area is the first step you should take before sitting down to meditate. If you don't already have an area designated for meditation, you'll need to create one. You want to organize, light candles, and burn incense. Collect any other meditation instruments you use, such as a shawl, Tibetan singing bowl, meditation chime, or japa mala beads. If you can't afford to have all those things that you don't need, just a simple, comfortable, and quiet place is enough to unblock your chakras and heal them. You just need an atmosphere that would allow you to connect to the spiritual side.

Get your body ready. Preparing your body is the second step in preparing for meditation. Take a relaxing bath, wash your face, brush your teeth, or do whatever else you need to do to make yourself feel clean and fresh before you sit. Check to see whether you're not thirsty or hungry or if you don't feel full enough. Make sure you are wearing comfortable attire before you sit down to meditate. Attend to any additional physical difficulties so that you can concentrate on your meditation.

Eliminate all distractions. Remove any distractions from the area, which is the third act to take. Turn off your phone. Feed the pets, use the restroom, and attend to any other bothersome problems or tasks that might interfere with or disturb your meditation.

Relax and unwind. If you want to release the tension you're carrying in your body, you may practice some yoga stretches or other motions. You should concentrate your stretches on the areas of your body that become achy and sore after prolonged sitting.

Take a seat. Keeping any support for your seated position is the fifth aspect of meditation preparation. Make sure all the items you could need, such as pillows, cushions, or blankets, are close at hand. Make sure you have more than you think you will need so that you won't have to stop to grab something in the middle of your meditation.

Set your goals. Reminding yourself of your goal or creating a new one for your practice is a potent approach to boosting success in meditation. The primary focus and objective of your meditation are these intentions. Just before you sit down to meditate, remind yourself of this to sharpen your attention and resolve.

Set the duration. It will be beneficial if you commit yourself fully to the practice. Making a decision regarding the duration of your meditation will also be important. It's crucial to decide how long you'll spend sitting before committing to a certain amount of time. It is simple to get distracted or quit your meditation early.

Set a timer in place. Using a timer is advised to assist you in sticking to a schedule of time. Find your timer and set it for any duration you would like before you sit.

Select your posture. Spend a little time letting yourself settle into your seated position as you prepare to meditate. Make any necessary corrections to your posture to ensure a long, tall spine and the least amount of muscular tension by supporting your body. A successful meditation practice requires a comfortable position.

Breathe more deeply. Finally, give yourself permission to relax into the sensation of your breath. Take deep and slow breaths. You might choose to use particular breathing techniques to either settle down or reenergize your body and mind if pranayama is a part of your practice. Try not to take up every item on this list at once if you are new to meditation. You could also want to test each one out to see how it affects your meditation practice. Allow yourself to develop kindness, compassion, and patience if you fail to remember any of these stages. Hopefully, developing a pre-meditation practice can help you focus more on the here and now and help your mind wander less.

Changing Old Habits

By forming new, healthier habits, breaking old bad habits might assist you in healing chakra imbalances. Changes in behavior and way of life assist us in breaking out of our daily thought and response habits. Chakra imbalances are usually resolved in part by changing our consciousness regarding ingrained assumptions about who we are and how we are connected to one another. Making ourselves aware of both the poor habit and the issue we are storing in a particular chakra is the first step to breaking old behaviors. When we become aware of problematic behavior or bad habit, we can either try to modify it or find alternative ways to react.

Think, for instance, about not standing up for yourself in a romantic setting. It may be a sign that your throat chakra is not aligned if you are unable to articulate your needs and desires. You might keep a mental note whenever you see yourself shutting down during a heated talk to break this behavior. When you become aware that you are stifling your own voice, pause and consider how you may respond otherwise, and apply the new response next. This objective will be achieved by any new reaction; however, effective, healthy reactions will be more beneficial than unhealthy or rash ones. Perhaps you decide to express how the contentious conversation made you feel to your partner in a way that they can hear you. By doing this, you assist in resolving the throat chakra's habit of silencing. We also modify the narrative to read "someone who works to communicate effectively" instead of "someone who keeps their lips shut." It takes time and effort to change one's consciousness around an established pattern. But after practicing it for a while, we can break bad habits and switch them to better ones.

This works because we actively engage in altering outdated routines by changing how we handle a reoccurring issue. We can remove outdated patterns and ideas that have been stored in particular chakras when we consistently practice for a long time.

How to Practice Chakra Meditation?

So how does one go about practicing a chakra meditation? It actually depends on the person because meditation evolves with each sitting. I advise using the hues related to each chakra as a focal point if you're a visual person. Others find it simpler to put a hand on each spot to express how they feel and to direct attention there while leading them through the meditation. Remember that meditation does not absolutely require closed eyes; while they are sometimes used to help you focus and soften your thoughts, candle meditation is one such technique. During the entire practice, you would sit with your eyes wide open, gazing at the flame. You may thus have a visual cue of the chakra points in front of you and, as you concentrate on each point, align it with the corresponding place on your own body, progressing from the root to the crown. I'd suggest acquiescing once you've reached the crown and closing your eyes.

If you prefer audio, then guided chakra meditations are wonderful since they usually specify not just the name of each chakra but also its location and color, allowing you to use visualization as you progress through the meditation. You can practice it every day or once a week, and you should attempt to meditate for about 20 minutes each time. There are two kinds of chakra meditation. Start concentrating on your breath as you lie flat on the floor or sit down. Close your eyes to draw your concentration within. Then draw your focus (in your imagination) to the first chakra point, the base, which represents your bond with the planet. And then think that you want this to be communicated to you in the most effective manner for you, whether that be the color we have been taught to identify with it, a symbol, or a word.

Step 1: Know your chakras. Recall everything you have read about the chakras and try to find each chakra according to the locations that were discussed in the previous "Chakra Overview" book. In order to unblock each chakra through meditation, you will have to imagine and think about those energy centers.

Step 2: Choose the correct environment. Make yourself comfortable in a silent, secluded space, whether inside or outside (aside from natural sounds). To avoid interruptions, turn off your doorbell and phone. Make sure your clothing is neither itchy nor excessively tight. So that you may focus on your body, close your eyes.

Step 3: Relax. Some experts advise doing meditation while standing, but you are welcome to sit or lie down on a cushion or a blanket. Breathe slowly and deeply, then relax your muscles.

Step 4: Go from bottom to top. It is important to identify the chakra that is blocked or otherwise off balance. Some problems can be connected to specific chakras, sometimes in ways that are clear beforehand. Always begin with the root chakra and end with the top crown chakra since doing so signifies moving from the body's most basic (survival) portion to its most advanced one (consciousness).

Step 5: Re-energize each chakra. A chakra might be visualized as a disc or lotus flower. As you inhale, picture light entering the chakra and filling it with vitality. When you exhale, visualize all of your stress leaving your chakra. If required, repeat, then continue on to the next chakra.

Step 6: Align chakras. Put simply, chakra alignment is getting them all to rotate in the same direction. Physical conditions or lying may be linked to a chakra that stops spinning or spins in the wrong direction. One approach to realign a chakra that is rotating in the wrong direction is to meditate while envisioning it spinning clockwise. Keep inhaling deeply after activating the crown chakra. Return to your daily activities as you slowly and calmly open your eyes.

The Deep Meditation Approach

For a newbie, chakra meditation can be quite intimidating at first. Consider using apps, websites dedicated to meditation, or even podcasts to receive guided chakra meditation if you feel you need assistance before trying it on your own. However, be sure to use materials from reputable and trustworthy sources in order to learn how to do it correctly. Here is a quick and easy chakra meditation technique.

1. Find a comfortable position. Seek out a location that is peaceful, reasonably cozy, and where you won't be bothered. Cross your legs in front of you while sitting upright. Place your hands freely on your knees. Use a meditation cushion if that seems like too much work.

2. Breathe deeply. Close your eyes and take several long breaths in and out to help you relax and concentrate.

3. Think about your chakras. Imagine an energy center with energy flowing through it, from the root chakra all the way up to the top of the head to the crown chakra. Make sure you comprehend each chakra's relationship to its related hue. Spend some time on each chakra. Give each chakra considerable time, and make sure that you can visualize energy flowing through each one. The chakra will become more apparent as you visualize a spinning wheel. Keep an eye on the direction of its flow, breathe into the light, shape, and space, and then just observe and trust. Watch how your breath heightens the chakra's glow and brilliance. The more vivid and bright, the better, as this is the cleansing. The mind will try to make you believe otherwise, but it is actually working. Imagine it turning clockwise and feel its warmth or coolness. Every breath that is sent out to enlarge and purify is a powerful source.

4. Visualize the chakra system in action as a whole. When you have completed all of the chakras, picture the entire chakra system with energy flowing smoothly from the root chakra to the crown chakra while having an impact on your body. Continue with each chakra in the same manner.

5. End your meditation. As you draw to a close, slowly open your eyes and pay attention to how you feel and how your body is energized.

Remember to follow your intuition and make note of where you need to spend more time. You should return to this area of work in your next session since certain points will expand easily while others will be more difficult. It's crucial to notice because you'll see every time you practice meditation how much you are changing on a daily, weekly, or monthly basis.

If you want to concentrate on a certain location that corresponds with where you want to concentrate emotionally, here is a second great technique. Start by concentrating on the chakra that you wish to focus your energies on the most. Let's use raising your voice as an illustration. You would need to use your throat chakra in this situation. You would start with your throat (the area right outside of your body). You would then add the mantra, "I am willing to release all that binds me; I allow myself to center and flow," and picture the wheel expanding with each breath.

Problems During Meditations

For beginners, meditation is not easy. It requires a lot of practice and concentration. During the first few sessions, you might experience some of the following problems. But don't worry—here are a few effective ways to tackle them:

Getting distracted during meditation and losing control. That's how your mind functions by nature. Count your breaths or repeat aloud to yourself a word or phrase (such as "peace" or "one") to help you cope. The goal of meditation practice is to transcend thought, not to stifle it. One technique to do this is to pay attention to your breath.

Falling asleep during meditation. When you're at ease and you feel relaxed, sleep comes naturally. When we let go of daily worries, it's normal to feel lethargic. Try sitting up when meditating if you feel sleepy. Remember to maintain a straight spine and try to keep your eyes open. Gently concentrate on a location a few feet in front of you.

Feeling Restless During a Meditation Session. Sitting still during meditation is a great challenge for me; what do I do? Make use of walking meditation: indoors or outside, stroll at your normal pace or more slowly. Breathing in rhythm with your steps will help. Look forward with a relaxed gaze and lowered eyes. Take note of how your feet are touching the ground. Pay attention to your breathing while walking.

Feeling pain in the back, knees, or neck during meditation. Your body may need to be adjusted, or you could simply be worn out. Keep in mind that you can meditate while seated or while lying down as long as you don't nod off. For most of us, just sitting motionless is a big challenge. Move to a more stable position if the discomfort is high. However, if it's only restlessness, attempt to stay with it. You might also want to give walking meditation a try.

Lack of time for regular meditation. You can carve out the time for it. Setting your alarm for a 15-minute earlier wake-up time or trying meditation as a pre-bedtime alternative to watching the late-night news. The most crucial step in learning how to begin meditating (and eventually developing a practice) is to routinely do it, even if it's only for ten minutes a day. All you require is consistency and a little time. Simply said, meditation can assist you in becoming more conscious and present. And that increases the enjoyment of life.

Not feeling any prominent change after the first few sessions of meditation. You can be stuck by your preconceived ideas about meditation. Just try to be more mindful of your breathing. Avoid having irrational hopes that something momentous will happen. In some ways, meditation is similar to a workout. Weightlifting repetitions aren't exactly fun, but you know the end result will be worthwhile. When all else fails, remember to be patient with yourself.

Your meditation practice is highly unique to you. Some individuals only need to become aware of the thoughts that have always rushed through their heads. Others experience great emotion while meditating. Others see meditation as a state of great concentration, while others experience it as a deeply relaxed yet extremely attentive state. In actuality, every person likely experiences all of these stages during a session, in addition to many others.

Meditation Poses

Quarter-Lotus Pose

If a primary school teacher instructed you to sit "crisscross," you would position yourself as a quarter lotus. Each foot is positioned below the opposing knee in this position. It resembles the standard cross-legged posture. In order to elevate the hips up and rotate the pelvis enough to prevent the lower back from arching while in this position, a meditation cushion is useful. To ensure a tilt, lean forward on the cushion. You should never keep your knees higher than your hips. Although it's ideal for your knees to rest softly against your feet, you can alter this to your liking.

If you've ever attended a meditation retreat, it's likely that you've observed other yogis using creative arrangements of zafus (round meditation cushions) and zabutons (larger square cushions that sit below the zafus) to create seating arrangements where the hips are raised much higher, as well as cushions below the legs and knees relieve pressure on the knees and ankles. The drawback of these meditation thrones is their instability. Try different things to find what works for you. You can buy meditation cushions online or use items you already have in your home (pillows, blankets, towels, etc.). You can always lean against a wall to brace your back. To assist with proper spine posture, try placing a rolled-up sweatshirt between the base of your lower back and the wall if you do this.

Half-Lotus Pose

With the exception of your left foot resting on top of your right thigh or vice versa, the half-lotus pose is identical to the quarter lotus pose. To prevent straining the knee joints when in the half-lotus position, you must have very flexible hips. If you have not spent much time on a yoga mat, this pose may be difficult for you. Try a yoga pigeon or reverse pigeon position as a warm-up if you need to prepare your body, especially if you have knee problems.

Full-Lotus Pose

For beginners, the posture when each foot is put upon the opposing thigh is known as the full-lotus position. Although it is very steady and symmetrical, which is advantageous to the mind-body connection, this meditation pose necessitates a lot of lower body flexibility.

If full lotus seems taxing on your body or you have knee or hip issues that make it risky, don't try it. This pose is made easier by yoga positions that expand the hips. However, forcing your body into a full-lotus position before it is ready will more likely result in physical therapy than blissful meditation.

Burmese Pose

In the Burmese position, both feet are placed in front of the pelvis. If you are flexible enough for your knees to naturally rest on the ground, it is a simple, relaxing position. Try leaning forward and back, left and right, and even squirming on the cushion while you sit (toward the front of the cushion) until you feel balanced and firmly anchored on your sitting bones. Your legs and feet will be under too much pressure if you lean too far forward.

Sitting in a Chair Pose

All the advantages of meditation are there whether you are sitting cross-legged or on a chair. Put your feet on the floor, shoulder-width apart, with your shins perpendicular to the surface. To get an upright spine, it's beneficial to sit closer to the edge of the chair. If necessary, you can lean against the chair back, but try to maintain proper posture at all times. Make the chair's back straight by adding a pillow or cushion as needed.

If you typically slouch while sitting, you might want to try placing a rolled-up sweatshirt between the chairback and the base of your lower back for support. A pillow or blanket can be placed on the chair to further tilt your hips and pelvis forward. If you can, set aside a chair solely for meditation. This acts as a cue from the environment; it's a method for the mind to develop the habit of realizing, "This is where I meditate." If you sit in the same chair for work or relaxation and meditate, it will be more difficult to mentally prepare.

Seiza Meditational Posture

Alternatively, you can kneel as is typical in Japanese culture. This practice, known as seiza, which translates to "right sitting," can be performed on a meditation bench, though a yoga block or cushion placed between your legs in a specific location can also work just as well. Without any assistance, you can also kneel while resting your legs solely on one another. The tops of the feet should be parallel to the surface.

Seiza's kneeling position eases the strain on the lower body's joints and aids the back's natural straightening out. For a beginner, some kind of padding beneath the knees and feet will be really helpful. If you sit on your heels and put your feet in the kiza position, with the balls of your feet facing forward, you will be performing another variation of the seiza pose. Although it's a terrific stretch for the bottom of the feet, it can be challenging for beginners to maintain.

Standing Meditation Position

Standing meditation is especially beneficial if you regularly nod off during your meditations or experience pain while you sit. You can stand while meditating using the same methods as when you sit. While standing, be careful not to lock your knees. If you are fatigued or having trouble focusing during your sitting practice, some teachers advise standing and performing a body scan meditation. If seated meditation positions are challenging or painful for you, you might also try walking meditation.

Lying Down Meditation

Any prolonged meditation session may cause some discomfort but lying down while you meditate is an alternative if even sitting in a chair causes you pain. Lay on your back in the corpse pose, also known as Savasana in yoga, with your arms at your sides and your palms up to meditate in this manner. To begin your meditation, try to maintain a steady, awake, and attentive body.

MEDITATION PRACTICES FOR EACH CHAKRA

An *outdoor meditation for the root chakra*. Do you feel balanced, anchored, safe, centered, and earthed? Your root chakra's secret is to, well, root. The root chakra can be balanced quickly by making a connection to the soil. I enjoy putting my bare feet on the ground to ground myself and balance my root chakra. I meditate on the earth's grounding energy while directing my attention to my feet, which serve as an anchor for my secure, centered body. Connecting to the soil is a rapid approach to balancing the root chakra. To balance my root chakra, I prefer to put my bare feet on the ground and feel myself grounding down. I enjoy meditating on the earth's grounding energy while directing my attention to my feet, which serve as an anchor for my secure and stable body.

A crystal meditation for the sacral chakra. Crystal and visualizations help to focus on this energy area. You must sever the cords with them in order to heal and clear obstructions surrounding the sacral chakra. Imagine yanking the cords at that center out of your body. After cutting the cords, sage your area. Then, instruct a carnelian crystal to assist you in bringing your sacral chakra into balance. Take three deep breaths while holding it in your hands and while closing your eyes. Say the following out loud or to yourself in your head: "I pray that the greatest frequency of love and light connect with my highest self to clear all undesirable energy and any prior training." This gemstone shall hold the intention of balancing, I order. I ask this crystal to keep my sacral chakra balance in mind. Place the crystal over your chakra for 11 minutes while lying comfortably on your back. Imagine the color orange covering every inch of your second chakra while it is on your body with a calming, balanced glow.

A morning visualization meditation for the solar plexus chakra. Try a little visualization just before you get out of bed if you feel like you could use some boost in your confidence. Your awareness of this energy area might be brought about by deep belly breathing. Take a few long, deep breaths while sitting down, feeling your stomach grow with each one. Once your body and breath have been brought into focus, start picturing how you will be moving through your day. Play through your list of tasks while visualizing how you would gracefully and easily get through the day. If you can complete this task outside on a bright day, then do it. If the sun is shining, I also prefer to walk outside and get some sunlight on that portion of my body. I visualize the sun's beams reaching my solar plexus and illuminating it.

A heart chakra yoga and meditation. Yoga is an excellent method for taking care of the heart. Shoulder flossing yoga, warrior 2, and a full wheel are heart-opening positions. Integrate these into a calming flow, and then complete the meditation thinking about all the things in life for which you are grateful to access that warm, fuzzy, loving energy.

Meditation boosters for the throat chakra. Anyone on this path to discovering and sharing their truth can benefit from the use of crystals and essential oils. I like using gems that balance the throat chakra, like blue lace agate, turquoise, or blue calcite. During meditation, you can hold it in your left hand because that hand absorbs the crystal's energy. Or, if it's tiny enough, you can meditate while lying down and position it at the base of your throat. The essential oils lavender, rosemary, frankincense, German chamomile, and hyssop are excellent choices for honoring our throat chakra.

A meditative session for the third-eye chakra. According to visualization specialists and instructors, mindfulness meditation is a means to improve our relationship with our own inner voice. They claim that meditation is the most effective approach to increasing our intuition and decreasing our fear. This energy center will flourish if you commit to daily meditation practice and ask yourself what you want to do for the day.

A guided meditation for the crown chakra. There is no better method to open up the seventh chakra than via meditation. Sit peacefully, with your back straight, either in a cozy chair with your feet flat on the ground or on the floor with your legs crossed.

The phrase "Roots down and hoist the crown" describes how to strengthen your seventh chakra from a balanced position by bringing your imagination roots from the base of the spine down into the earth and rising your crown upward. Your core is the vertical line that connects the centers of your base and crown chakras. As you meditate, this helps you stay grounded and in the present. Then picture breathing as a lightening that rises up from your center on inhalation and falls back down on exhale. This strengthens the Sushumna, or center line, as it is known in yoga.

Then visualize opening your crown chakra like the lotus flower with a thousand petals, which is its emblem. In the same way, a flower takes in the sunshine, take in the energy of grace, consciousness, or guidance. Pull it down through the crown into the body. Pull it all the way to the roots of the core, down the stem. Realizing there is an endless source of light, continue to take it in a while, letting your mind wander and your body fills with light. When your mind is still, and you feel as though your entire body is being filled with bright white light, keep picturing light pouring into your crown. Stay as long as you can, bask in the magnificence of that brightness and stillness.

Take your time when you're ready to end the meditation. Instead, exercise a dual concentration, keeping one eye on the inside while the other is on the outside so that you can preserve your radiant state as you return to the outside world and your daily routines.

HEAL WITH YOGA

Yoga's core belief is that the mind, body, and spirit are all interconnected and cannot be clearly distinguished from one another. The deeper aspects of the body, mind, and spirit can, nevertheless, be explored using a wide range of philosophical concepts. To change our perception of ourselves as distinct and to realize the unitive condition, it is crucial to study and comprehend these concepts.

Philosophy of Yoga

Similar to Buddhism, yoga philosophy holds that pain is caused by spiritual ignorance, which keeps us trapped on the wheel of samsara (cycle of rebirth). Yoga offers a variety of ways to eradicate our ignorance. However, the main tenets of yoga's philosophy are the development of mental discernment, detachment, spiritual knowledge, and self-awareness.

The various yoga traditions make use of various facets of Upanishadic non-dualism and Sankhya dualism. Some spiritual practices, such as tantra and Bhakti, make use of the gods and goddesses of Hinduism. In addition, Ishvara, a personal god, is mentioned in Patanjali's yoga sutras. As a result, a yogi needs to comprehend the connections between the Atman and the Brahman, the Prakriti and the Purusha, as well as the trinity of Brahma, Vishnu, and Shiva.

The concept of karma serves as the cornerstone of yoga philosophy. The thing that divides our ego from our unitive consciousness of the cosmos is illusion or ignorance, known as Maya. Our karma makes it possible for us to be connected to the wheel of samsara, which prolongs our suffering and the illusion of Maya. These fundamental worldviews can be perplexing to Westerners, but they are useful in helping us realign our thinking so that we can recognize and feel the interconnectedness of all things. The subtle body and the passage of prana and kundalini spiritual energies through the nadis and chakras are other ideas that are incorporated into yoga philosophy. This energy anatomy serves as a solid theoretical grounding for hatha yoga.

A sustained state of pure awareness, known as Moksha or Samadhi, is the ultimate aim of yoga. In order to achieve one's true self or highest self, one does yoga. Our fundamental nature is this sensation of unadulterated consciousness. All philosophical and mental structures disintegrate in this liberated state. In essence, learning about yogic philosophy is essential for developing one's yoga practice and realizing enlightenment.

Yoga postures cannot be categorized in a single fashion, although there are thirteen main physical orientations that can be used to investigate and order asanas. These categories of yoga positions will typically have comparable energetic and physical benefits. You may improve and develop your yoga practice by being aware of the advantages of each type of asana.

How does it work? Yoga aids in awakening and opening the chakras by bringing vital life power into them. In general, yoga uses a sensory experience to help us become more physically rooted. This is particularly helpful for those of us who tend to spend more time mentally preoccupied than rooted in the energy of the planet or truly present in our physical bodies. It also highlights how our postures influence how we move about the environment. For instance, when we are sad, we have the propensity to hunch our shoulders forward and move our bodies in a concave manner. We do this to safeguard our heart chakra in terms of our energy body. However, if we maintain this position for an extended period of time, it may result in the upper back or shoulder pain. Yoga practice enables us to become conscious of the tension in our shoulders and upper back, interact with it, and, finally, let it go.

Benefits of yoga. Yoga can be a great type of fitness because it involves a lot of physical activity. Yoga courses are usually held in serene studios, making them calming and excellent for reducing stress. Some people discover that yoga aids in the practice of improved eating habits and other positive lifestyle changes since it cultivates awareness of the body. Moreover, not a lot of pricey equipment is typically needed for yoga.

Yoga And Prana

Yoga practitioners should strive to comprehend their vital energy and develop a sensitivity to it for a number of reasons. In order to know how and when to modify or change these practices, it is crucial to have a feedback mechanism because many yogic activities either create or alter the energy in our bodies. There are numerous benefits to exercising, increasing our energy awareness and sensitivity as we practice:

- It guides more subtle modifications to yoga positions' physical alignment.
- It develops vigor and strength to perform yoga asanas and other yoga practices both physically and intellectually.
- It gives us information on the results of a series of positions and can help us decide which poses to use.
- It develops the capacity for recovery and well-being.
- It serves as the basis for pranayama breathing exercises and offers insight into the effectiveness of these methods.
- It can let us know if we've been successful in establishing and keeping a yogic lifestyle.
- It aids in grounding our awareness in the here and now.
- It interferes with the nature and quantity of our thoughts, which hinders our capacity for meditation.

There are many different types and poses of yoga, but the one that is most usually practiced focuses on asana, a series of physical positions and breathing techniques said to improve our physical, mental, and spiritual well-being. Asana is a set of exercises meant to build physical stamina and strength while also promoting awareness of and connection to the body through movement. Yoga poses are a fantastic way to alter oneself physically, mentally, and spiritually. We link the mind with the tissues of our body through physical activity and breathing. Numerous yoga poses aid in opening up different areas of the body, which raises chakra awareness and balance. When performing yoga asanas, we move the body into different physical positions and hold them for predetermined amounts of time. We simultaneously control our breathing in various ways, promoting mindfulness and assisting the body's energy flow. There are many types of yoga, and some of them can be very beneficial for chakra balancing. For instance, kundalini yoga attempts to awaken the kundalini energy that flows through our chakras by chanting, breathing exercises, and meditation.

Yoga Poses

Yoga must be practiced in conjunction with self-study and the development of calm to truly help chakra healing, and it takes time to achieve the best benefits. Advanced yoga poses should only be performed under the direct supervision of a certified yoga instructor because they carry a higher risk of injury (headstand and shoulder stand, for instance, are not recommended for beginners or anybody who has recently sustained a neck injury). Based on the body position and alignment pattern, asanas, which are poses or positions in which the body is supported by the ground or another object, can be divided into broad categories. The majority of the following asanas are used by yoga instructors in their hatha yoga sessions.

Standing pose. Any hatha yoga practice must start with standing poses. They help us prepare for deeper stretches and more difficult positions by increasing our body's strength and flexibility throughout. Standing positions activate the muscles across the entire body, warming the body. We must be mindful of how our feet, knees, hips, spine, and head are positioned as we stand. We risk hurting ourselves if we don't align these parts properly.

Standing yoga poses, which are a key element of well-rounded yoga practice, call for both flexibility and strength. Standing positions tend to be stimulating and open and are usually held for shorter durations than other poses, typically only two to four breaths long. These are the most difficult postures; therefore, beginners should proceed with caution. Beginner students should first concentrate on the fundamental poses because they comprise many of the more difficult asanas.

Standing poses have a number of advantages. Strong and sturdy legs, hips, and core muscles are typically developed through standing poses, including Mountain, Tree and the five Warrior postures. Standing poses like Triangle Pose and Warrior 1, have the arms lifted, help to develop upper body strength and flexibility. These stances ground us and make us feel solid and resilient. They also support our connection to the earth's element that resides within us.

Sitting yoga. The majority of seated asanas, which are the most prevalent, are appropriate for beginning students. The majority of seated yoga poses emphasize flexibility over strength and tend to be more energetically grounded. Sitting on the floor gives a steady position that makes it easier to relax and open the body. They are simple to modify for any strength and flexibility level. They also assist us in becoming conscious of the breath and its impact on the body. Moreover, they help us sit up straighter by activating our core muscles. Stretching the quadriceps, hamstrings, calves, and back body to increase flexibility and range of motion is very beneficial when performing seated poses. Because of their stability, low center of gravity, and control, they also present a lesser danger of injury.

Supine poses. Yoga supine poses are performed while resting on your back. Because they involve less balance and coordination than standing positions, these postures are typically simpler to execute. Stress is released and flexibility is enhanced by prone positions. They are integrating, supporting, relaxing, nurturing, and cooling. They are excellent for unwinding the body and mind, and they are helpful for easing stress and tension in the shoulders, neck, and back. People who struggle with anxiety or insomnia may find them especially beneficial.

By performing asanas while lying on your back, you may make use of gravity to strengthen your backbends and increase the flexibility in your spine and legs. After a lengthy practice, supine poses are ideal for relaxing. These poses are usually taught by yoga instructors toward the end of a class. They give us time to relax the spine and limbs and to think back on the lessons we have learned from practice. While some people choose to use them to unwind before going to sleep, others find them to be tranquil and calming. Regardless, these positions are excellent ways to wrap up your practice and get ready for Shavasana.

Twist poses. Twisting yoga poses are usually employed to alleviate back strain and improve overall body flexibility. The muscles that support your back are strengthened and lengthened by them. After a series of backbends or forward bends, twists are excellent neutralizing poses that help the body adjust. Moreover, they can strengthen our abdominal muscles, open our hips, and enhance digestion.

Twists reach deep into the body's center to release poisons from the internal organs and replenish them with new, oxygenated blood. They also promote mentally letting go of unhelpful things. Twisting exercises can enhance coordination, core strength, and physical balance. Twists let go of chest tension and expand the lungs. They are also excellent for reducing stress, clarifying the mind, and enhancing vitality and energy.

Balancing positions. Yoga positions that involve balancing are typically performed while standing on one foot, which calls for more stability and core power than other poses. Strength, balance, and focus can all be improved with balancing poses. They can help support and strengthen the back, neck, arms, and legs. In addition to preventing falls and injuries, balancing poses are helpful for enhancing posture and raising awareness of how we stand and move.

For people who wish to work on improving their balance, body awareness, and coordination, balancing postures are very helpful. These poses develop self-assurance, tenacity, and resolve while strengthening and energizing the intellect. They also aid in improving our concentration, strengthening our sense of self, and becoming more conscious of our breathing. The purpose of practicing balancing poses in the middle of a sequence is to make use of their energizing and revitalizing effects to move deeper into more difficult and advanced postures. Although tough, balancing poses gets easier with practice. The secret is perseverance, attention, and consistency.

Postures to improve your core. It may be time to add some core-strengthening yoga poses to your regimen if you're seeking strategies to increase your general level of fitness and prevent injury. They assist us to steady ourselves when we stand or sit by strengthening the abs. Moreover, they strengthen the muscles that keep the hips and pelvis stable, reducing the risk of lower back pain and injury. These postures lengthen the hamstrings and expand the hips to increase flexibility in addition to strengthening the body.

Yoga positions that strengthen the core lower the chance of falling during practice, which could result in injury. Asanas that strengthen your core make you feel stronger, more self-assured, and better equipped to perform challenging postures. Moreover, they assist us in achieving greater general alignment in our poses and strengthen our mental toughness and resilience.

Bending forward poses. The front of the upper torso is brought closer to the lower body in forwarding folds. Forward bends are thought to be introspective, peaceful, and tranquil. They loosen up the entire backside of the body's tense and stiff muscles. They can ease fatigue, headaches, stress, and other symptoms of depression and anxiety.

It's crucial to take your time and practice a forward bend yoga pose with the right alignment and consciousness. Don't push or pull your body into the posture. Instead of pushing and forcing yourself further into the pose, put your attention on relaxing and melting into it. If you experience any pain while performing a forward fold, keep your back flat and stretch your spine.

Try knee-bending forward bends if you have tight hamstrings. Use a series of blocks for support and to help stretch the spine if it is hard for you to reach your hands to the floor. Place a blanket or pillow under your hips when you are seated to help keep your lower back from curving. Straps can also be used to assist in getting to your feet.

Backbend positions. Because they stretch the spine, reduce lower back stress, and enhance posture, backbends are among the most crucial movements in a yoga sequence. They awaken prana, raise blood pressure, improve mood, and awaken the heart chakra. Backbends are excellent for opening up the front body and offer a wonderful chance to concentrate on breathing. Any back pain you have could be the result of tense muscles or bad posture. Try to locate a seat that is cozy so you can unwind your neck and shoulders. You can then inhale deeply into your belly without putting any tension on your upper body. Backbends might be difficult to perform if you spend most of your days sitting at a computer since they call for a certain amount of mobility in the hips and lower back.

A solid base for your backbends is created by digging deep into your hands, knees, or hips. Using the belly lock, or Uddiyana Bandha, helps to protect the spine and stabilize it. Pulling the navel toward the spine and elevating the pubic bone away from the tailbone will activate the Uddiyanna Bandha. This will fortify the abdominal wall and lessen lower back pain.

Opening hip poses. Yoga poses that extend the hips and aid in stretching the six muscular groups that move the hip joint are referred to as hip-opening poses. These generally involve floor positions that support the body's weight to promote deeper stretching. Although hip openers are usually performed following a warm-up or cool-down session, some people choose to perform them before beginning their yoga routine.

Yoga poses that open the hips are a great way to loosen up the tight hamstrings and hip flexors that are sometimes brought on by prolonged sitting. Moreover, they aid in enhancing balance and posture, reducing stress, increasing flexibility, lowering the risk of injury (particularly to the lower back), and enhancing range of motion in the hips, legs, and back. They are a wonderful addition to other athletic activities like jogging, cycling, and dancing.

Hip openers can be used to improve strength and mobility throughout the hips, knees, and ankles. They tend to be energetically rooted and concentrate more on flexibility than strength. Since the majority of hip-opening asanas are easily modified to accommodate any level of strength or flexibility, they are excellent for new yoga students.

Side bend poses. Yoga postures known as side bends concentrate on the side body. They work wonders to ease tension in the torso's sides, shoulders, and arms. Yoga side bends are excellent for widening the chest and rib cage. We can feel the energy flowing through our bodies as we breathe into these stretches, letting go of any tension and opening up the places where we hold ourselves back.

Side bends are particularly beneficial for calming the mind, opening the lungs, and restoring nervous system equilibrium. Side bends are beneficial for improving flexibility, spinal mobility, and core strength. Moreover, they improve stamina, endurance, focus, and memory. Side bends strengthen the lungs, increase circulation, improve energy levels, and promote immunity with frequent exercise.

Reversals. Asanas known as inversions place the head below the level of the hips and heart. Aside from less evident asanas like downward dog or a standing forward fold, these poses typically involve being upside down or inverted from your normal upright stance.

Practicing yoga inversions is one of the finest methods to energize the nervous system, boost the immune system, and enhance general health. The entire musculoskeletal system, including the back, neck, legs, and arms, can benefit from inversions by becoming stronger. Moreover, these poses enhance memory, clarity of thought, mood, and self-worth. Blood flow and lymphatic drainage are naturally enhanced by body inversion, which reduces inflammation.

Poses for meditation. Specific seated positions, known as meditation poses, are employed during breathing exercises and meditation techniques. These only contain a few asanas, but as they are usually taught at the start and conclusion of yoga class, they are crucial to master. It's critical to stretch your spine and preserve your lumbar region's natural curve in any meditation stance. If you notice that you're rounding forward, sit up straight and raise your hips with a pillow or bolster.

During meditation, a relaxed seated position should remove or lessen pain. Your chakras will be encouraged to be open and balanced by a posture with a long and erect spine. During meditation, it is very beneficial to have an open heart to promote a caring and loving energy flow. In addition, you will feel more energized, focused, and relaxed if you maintain appropriate alignment in these positions.

Putting the various yoga poses in order. Balance, harmony, and tranquility within oneself are the aims of yoga. A series of yoga postures can be put together in a certain order to achieve this equilibrium. Although each yoga posture has its own special advantages, they are usually combined with other poses of the same kind. Therefore, in order to receive better results, it is best to practice sets of them together.

Yoga Poses for Each Chakra

Finding the physical postures that feel correct for you is ultimately the most crucial step. Yoga can be practiced in a variety of ways, but there is only one way to feel fantastic. Yoga encourages you to play about and experiment to see what works best for you.

Mountain Pose for Root Chakra

Put your feet together and keep your arms by your sides as you stand. The balls and arches of your feet should bear the same amount of your weight. Consistently and rhythmically breathe. Stand with your feet six inches apart if you have problems balancing (or wider). Legs should be straight, heels should be drawn down, and feet should be firmly planted on the ground. Pull your quadriceps up and back. Do not round your lower back; instead, slightly tuck in your tailbone. Keep your hips aligned with your body's centerline.

Extend through your torso as you inhale. Pull your shoulder blades back toward the back of your waist as you exhale. Keep both your shoulders in line with the sides of your body as you open out at the collarbone. Do not push your shoulder blades together as you press them toward your back ribs. Keep your triceps tight, arms stretched and straight. Stretch out your neck. Maintain steady, calm breathing throughout, yes at ease. For as long as a minute, hold.

Warrior II for Sacral Chakra

Keep your feet wide apart as you stand on your yoga mat. Turn your left foot slightly inward while keeping your right foot toward the top of the mat. Reach out energetically from fingertip to fingertip while raising your arms, so they are parallel to the ground. Aim to keep your front knee bent over your ankle at90-degrees. Your left foot's outside edge should be used to press back. Keep your torso parallel to the ground while widening across your collarbones and expanding the space between your shoulder blades. Look across your right middle finger as you draw your tailbone slightly downward. Hold up to a minute. Repeat on the opposite side.

Plank Pose for Solar Plexus Chakra

With your wrists directly beneath your shoulders, start out on your hands and knees. Fingers spread, use your forearms and hands to press downward. Keep your chest from collapsing. With your neck extended and your abdominal muscles pulled toward your spine, look down. Bring your body and head into a straight line by tucking your toes and taking a step back with your feet. Keep your thighs raised and watch out for letting your hips drop too far. Realign your whole body so that your shoulders are squarely above your wrists if your buttocks protrude into the air.

As you tighten your abdominal muscles, draw your pelvic floor muscles toward your spine. Try raising one leg at a time to intensify the posture. After holding for five breaths, carefully drop your entire body to the ground and relax.

Camel Pose for Heart Chakra

Start by kneeling up straight with your knees at hip width. As you press your shins and the tops of your feet into the ground, rotate your thighs inward. With your fingers pointing down to the floor, keep your hands on the back of your pelvis. Take each heel in your hands as you lean back. Your thumbs should be holding the outside of each foot. Without tensing your shoulder blades, extend your arms outward. Maintain a neutral head position or let your head droop. Hold up to a minute. Bring your hands back to your front to release. Take a deep breath, lead with your heart, and then lift up your torso by lowering your hips to the ground. Your head should be the last to rise.

Bridge Pose for Throat Chakra

With your legs bent and feet kept flat on the yoga mat, lie on your back. As you elevate your hips toward the ceiling, firmly plant your feet and arms into the ground. Maintain parallel thighs and feet. Clasp your hands, extend your arms along the yoga mat beneath your hips, and roll your shoulders back and underneath your torso. For as long as a minute, hold. One vertebra at a time, softly roll your spine to the floor to relax.

Tree Pose for Third Eye Chakra

Start out in mountain pose (Tadasana). Move your weight slightly to your left foot. Reach down and grab your right ankle while bending your right knee. Draw your right foot next to your inner left thigh using your hand. Only lay your foot above or below your knee, not against it. Lengthen your tailbone toward the floor while placing your hands on your hips. Softly fix your gaze in front of you. Put your left thigh against your right foot. Stretch your arms above your head and point your fingertips upwards for a deeper position. Try closing your eyes to intensify your stance. For as long as a minute, hold. Return to the initial position and repeat on the other side.

Corpse Pose for Crown Chakra

Close your eyes as you lay on your back. You might wish to wrap a blanket around your body. Give yourself permission to feel heavy on the earth. Allow your arms and legs to hang open. Release every body part, organ, and cell, starting at the bottom of your feet and working your way up to the top of your crown chakra. Allow your eyes to close tightly. Bring inner stillness and silence into your body, mind, and spirit. Spend a total of five to fifteen minutes in Savasana. Then, breathe more deeply while gently moving your body and regaining awareness of it. Do a right-side roll. Take a deep breath and situate yourself comfortably in a sitting position. Take the tranquility you've established with you for the remainder of the day.

The Don'ts of Meditation and Yoga

Spiritual ignorance. Even though it may feel pleasant at the moment, bypassing our emotions makes our practice less effective and hinders our spiritual development. How do you stop bypassing? When practicing, make sure you are anchored in your body and in your center. Connect with your feelings and allow your practice to embrace them rather than push them away. You may not be grounded enough and may be in the bypass area if you are experiencing too many "out of body" experiences.

Using shortcuts. Although you can meditate while driving, doing the dishes, or gardening, formal practice time is crucial to sustaining your meditation practice sessions. Don't rush through these periods of practice. Schedule at least an hour without interruptions to sit in meditation in order to experience the full effect of spiritual awakening. A clock can be placed in front of you to stop you from cutting the exercise short. Formal practice develops gradually over time, much like a vision quest. You need enough time to clear your mind of the hustle and bustle of the outside world, travel through your emotions, and discover the essence of who you are. At each fifteen-minute interval of practice, you can see a change, which can give you more drive to continue.

Not practicing. Obviously, practicing meditation makes it more effective. Despite our best efforts, how frequently do we actually manage to carve out time for our practice? Remind yourself that you will only be sitting for two minutes before getting up. Even if you do get up after two minutes, you will feel terrific. However, once you start practicing, your nervous system starts to feel the effects, and you naturally want to keep going. Sometimes, meditation is more calming and restorative than sleep. Make use of this tip to continue your meditation practice regularly.

Following gimmicky versions. Traditional meditation has numerous contemporary versions. Several of them can muddy the practice. Many gimmicky modern meditations are created by teachers who lack in-depth spiritual training and believe their reinvention of the wheel is superior to what is already available. Remember that traditional schools of training have thousands of years of experience teaching meditation and seeing students develop through the practice. Although the past 200 years of science have much to offer, spiritual development is an age-old endeavor. Gimmicky meditation can occasionally be enjoyable to grab our attention and remind us of the value of mind training, but if you're a serious practitioner, beware of these contemporary innovations and stick to the old and time-tested methods.

Day vs. night. Daytime meditation is beneficial. It may be best to meditate in the morning and at night. It is preferable to meditate in the middle of the night. There is a special reason why so many monks get up at night to practice. It is the quietest time to meditate. There is nothing happening. Nothing further needs to be done. Without interruptions, you can focus deeply. Meditating at three in the morning feels different from doing it during the day. You'll observe how your body absorbs the energy of the environment and the action going on around you. Compared to midday meditation, delving deeper can be easier in the early morning and right before going to sleep. But a particularly beautiful moment to practice is the middle of the night.

Using too many props. Be careful not to rely on the meditation props too much. The goal of meditation is to achieve self-comfort and satisfaction with one's inner experience of life. To that aim, it can be beneficial to sit by yourself and have to face who you are right now, as you entered this planet, empty-handed. A cluttered environment can make it difficult to experience your true nature. Some individuals, for instance, may have their pillow, their beads, their sacred water, their altar, a candle, ideal lighting, another individual, etc. If they lack those items, practice becomes challenging. Consider minimizing the number of props in your practice if you don't require more than a few things to keep you awake or focused. Try meditating alone in the dark without any tools or music. This test is worthwhile.

BOOK 3:
HEALING REMEDIES AND TREATMENTS

Yoga and meditation are not the only two ways to heal your chakras. Everything that we consume affects the energies within us. So, by drinking, eating, and inhaling things that are beneficial for our chakras, we can ensure their healing. In addition to supporting your physical body, food may also support your energy body. Eating certain foods can promote the energetic healing of your chakras. What you eat and drink matters when it comes to chakra health since your energy body and physical body are intertwined. Water consumption can have an impact on our health. Making better eating decisions can significantly contribute to your body's recovery and raise the energy of your chakras. Your physical health improves when you consume more clean meals, which are those that are less processed, more sustainably harvested, seasonally available, organic, locally sourced, and created with fewer additives and more complete components. Your energy body also gains when your physical body does. Clean eating promotes the physical and mental well-being of your body. All of your body's systems benefit from raising your awareness of foods that are good for you and those that are not — for instance, through stimulating cell growth; bone growth; muscle, organ, and gland health; and mental processes. All of this consequently boosts your energy body. There are numerous possibilities and choices for nourishing your physical and energetic bodies with food, and when you use them, it may be helpful for both of them.

Herbalism is a widely accepted therapy that suggests the intake of different plants or their extracts to heal different ailments in the body. Since healing our life force, or prana, and unblocking the chakras is the goal here, in this book, I am sharing some of the most used and time-tested herbal remedies and aromatherapy treatments to unblock any chakra in your body.

HEALING REMEDIES

There are several healing remedies that you can try besides meditation and yoga to heal your chakras. Our chakras are affected by the functioning of our body and our surroundings, so by introducing things into your life that are beneficial for each chakra, you can ensure their healing. In this chapter, I am sharing several of my time-tested chakra healing remedies, which can broadly be categorized into herbal tea therapy, aromatherapy, therapy through crystals, and reiki, along with acupuncture remedies. The great thing about these remedies is that they are simple and easy to follow, and you won't need anyone else's help to try them. You will have to buy a few herbs, some useful crystals, and essential oils, and that is it! Use them regularly, along with meditation and yoga, for amazing results.

Burdock Root Tea for Root Chakra

This ground root is an excellent cleansing and detoxifying agent because it is proven to remove pollutants from our internal ecology. Its potent metabolic profile also aids in shielding us from free radicals, which have the potential to prevent a number of diseases, including cancer.

Ingredients:

- 8 to10 burdock root strips
- 2 C. filtered water
- 1 tsp. organic honey or sugar

First, get fresh burdock root strips to make your burdock root tea. They should first be cut into slices of one to two inches. Then, using a potato peeler or knife, peel the root chunks into thin strips that may resemble bark peelings. Put this outside to dry for three to four hours in the sun.

After they have dried, put them in a cooking pan without any oil, and heat them up. If you heat them for five to ten minutes, they will roast. A rich, golden-brown color is what you want. They can be cooked into burdock root tea once they have cooled. The surplus should be kept in a Mason jar and kept in a cool, dark, and dry location for future use.

To make the tea, put burdock root strips in a teapot. Pour water into a stainless-steel kettle and heat it to a boil. After removing the stainless-steel pot from the heat, give it a couple of minutes to cool. Pour this water into the teapot after that. Give the mixture five to ten minutes to steep. Strain and pour the tea after that, sweeten it with any natural sweeteners, and then drink it.

Fennel Tea for Sacral Chakra

Fennel is prized for its ability to inspire bravery, fend off bad spirits, and balance the sacral chakra. But more than that, by reducing gas and bloating, this lovely post-meal companion supports a healthy digestive system.

Ingredients:

- 1/2 tsp. honey
- 1 Tbsp. crushed fennel seeds
- 1 1/2 C. water
- 1/4 in. crushed lightly ginger
- 3 mint leaves

Add 1 ½ C. of water to any suitable cooking pot. Heat it to a boil. Then add crushed ginger and fennel seeds to the pot. When the water has been reduced to 1 C., simmer it on medium heat. After that, turn off the heat and pour the tea into a cup. Blend in honey thoroughly. Your fennel tea is now prepared for consumption. You can add mint leaves as a garnish. Enjoy.

Ginger Tea for Solar Plexus

Ginger tea has numerous chemicals that can assist the body take up glucose, which is beneficial if you battle type 2 diabetes, in addition to being a natural cure for nausea and indigestion. Balanced emotional response and your capacity to establish appropriate boundaries are supported energetically by this.

Slice your fresh ginger very thinly. It doesn't need to be peeled beforehand, but you should clean it and scrape off any visible dirt. For each cup of tea, use a piece of ginger that is about an inch long. Combine the ginger with new water in a saucepan (use 1 C. of water per serving).

Over high heat, heat the tea mixture to a boil. To keep the temperature at a moderate simmer, lower the heat as needed. Simmer for five minutes\ (or up to ten minutes if you want extra-strong tea). To remove all of the ginger, pour the tea through a fine strainer. If you'd like to add some complimentary acidity to your tea, serve it with a thin round of lemon or orange. Add some honey or maple syrup to control the spicy ginger flavor, if needed.

Tulsi Tea for Heart Chakra

In Ayurvedic medicine, this heart-opener is referred to as "holy basil" and is regarded as the most sacred herb in India. Tulsi is a useful plant that improves longevity, lowers anxiety, and even aids in the treatment of acne. Its leaves include eugenol, which has potent anti-microbial qualities and increases your capacity for compassion, as well as ursolic acid and carvacrol.

Ingredients:

- 1 tsp. Tulsi fresh leaves, or ½ tsp. dried
- 1½ C. water
- 1 tsp. lemon juice
- 1 tsp. honey

Heat the water to a full boil in any suitable pot. Add the Tulsi leaves after that. Cook for about ten to fifteen minutes at a medium temperature, stirring occasionally. Use a sieve to filter the tea. Mix thoroughly after adding the honey and lemon juice. Enjoy.

Ashwagandha Tea for Throat Chakra

This well-liked Ayurvedic herb, also known as ashwagandha, is referred to as an adaptogen. This adaptogenic plant is a natural ally if you experience persistent fatigue, a slow thyroid, or adrenal problems because they help your body deal with stress effectively. It will also increase throat strength, which will assist you in clearing this center if you need a little assistance in expressing your views.

Ingredients:

- 1 C. of water
- 1 tsp. Ashwagandha roots
- Half lemon
- Honey to taste

Heat water to a boil in any suitable pot. Close the lid and turn off the heat after adding the Ashwagandha roots. Give it ten to fifteen minutes to steam or infuse. Put a cup of it through a strainer, then add honey and lemon juice.

Lavender Tea for Third Eye Chakra

Drinking lavender tea, which is known for its capacity to open the third eye, will ease restlessness, relax the nervous system, and support your sleep schedule. It has a reputation for helping to cure melancholy and mood swings by regulating mood.

Ingredients:

- 1 C. water
- 2 Tbsp. dried lavender

In a small saucepan, combine the water and lavender. Boil for a moment, then turn down the heat to simmer and cook for three minutes. After removing from the heat, steep for twenty to thirty minutes. Then strain after cooling to room temperature.

Gotu Kola for Crown Chakra

Gotu Kola, a plant grown in the Himalayas, is used by yogis to enhance meditation. The growth of the crown chakra is considered to be facilitated by Gotu Kola's ability to balance the two hemispheres of the brain. This rejuvenating herb aids in the medical treatment of your nervous system, blood pressure regulation, bloodstream detoxification, and improved sleep.

You can use fresh, dried, or powdered leaves and stems to make this herbal tea. All that's left to do is begin brewing the tea.

Get your teapot and cups, then heat the water in the kettle. Put 1 tsp. Of dried, fresh, or crushed Gotu Kola leaves per cup of water in the teapot. Replace the lid on the teapot after adding the boiling water.

Allow the herbs to steep for ten to fifteen minutes. Keep in mind that the longer you let the herbs simmer, the stronger the tea will be. It might be advisable to start out with brief infusions.

Although the tea is generally good on its own, strain it into a cup, then add honey if desired. Some claim that Gotu Kola tea has an earthy, slightly parsley-like flavor. Enjoy your tea while it's still hot.

You can only consume three cups every day for a period of six weeks. It is advised that you start with one cup of weak tea each day and increase your intake from there because you might initially experience some nausea or stomachache.

WEEKLY HERBAL PLAN

Since there are seven days a week, we can schedule our daily care for each chakra to keep all of them in balance.

Monday

Ginger Latte

You can have this latte any time of the day, although the best way to start your day is to have it in the morning. Regular intake of this latte will revitalize you in the long run. Here is how you can make it:

Ginger syrup

1 ½ C. filtered water

1 C. organic cane sugar

1 C. roughly chopped fresh ginger

Latte

1 to2 Tbsp. ginger syrup

1 1/4 C. unsweetened plain almond milk

Ginger tea (optional)

Ginger powder or cinnamon powder

To make the ginger syrup, bring the water, sugar, and ginger to a boil in a suitable pan while stirring to dissolve the sugar. Cook for a further forty-minutes after lowering the heat to a gentle simmer. For simple storage, pour the cooked mixture through a fine mesh strainer into a bottle or jar.

Next, to make the ginger latte, heat the almond in any suitable skillet or microwave. Then, add 1 to 2 Tbsp. of ginger syrup. If necessary, taste and adjust sweetness. Before adding syrup, simmer a ginger tea packet in almond milk for three to five minutes for even more ginger taste. Add some cinnamon, ginger powder, or your other favorite spices before serving.

The ginger syrup lasts up to a month if it is stored in the refrigerator. You can also use this latte as a ginger-infused sweetener in cocktails or to make ginger soda when combined with tonic water.

Tuesday

Calendula Tea

There are many advantages of using calendula. It has remarkable healing qualities that make it great for the skin, treating conditions like eczema, diaper rash, and simple aging. Moreover, calendula tea has antiviral qualities that can aid with conditions like viral pink eye, and antifungal qualities that can assist with yeast infections or athlete's foot. Here is how you can make calendula tea:

2 Tbsp. Calendula blossoms (dry or fresh)

1 C. boiling water

Put 2 Tbsp. of dried or fresh calendula flowers in a cup.

Heat 1 C. of water to a boil in any pot or kettle and pour it over the flowers.

Leave the calendula to steep for 10 to 15 minutes with a cover on.

Strain the calendula tea using a fine sieve and pour it into the serving cup to serve warm. You can also serve it cold as iced tea.

Wednesday

Rosemary Tea

Rosemary tea is an amazing herbal drink to consume because it has several health advantages. It has antimicrobial qualities and is high in antioxidants. It's a terrific tea to drink if you're starting to feel that you are catching a cold or are simply seeking healthier beverage options. To make this tea, you can either use fresh or dried rosemary. Use 1 tsp. of finely chopped rosemary and let it steep for a few minutes, depending on your preferred level of flavor.

2 to 3 tsp. rosemary leaves

2 C. boiling water

Put the rosemary in hot boiling water and let it steep for five minutes. The tea will be stronger the longer you leave it. (Too long will make it bitter.) If you're using fresh leaves, you may either strain them out or keep them in while you drink. I advise filtering them out if you're using dried rosemary. For a sweet taste, you can add some honey to the tea as well.

Thursday

Jasmine Tea

Jasmine is said to have many health benefits. It can boost energy, help in weight loss, support cancer prevention and heart health protection, relieve stress, prevent type 2 diabetes, help improve the immune system, and work against inflammation. It is also beneficial to the skin. For jasmine tea, you have two options: either prepare jasmine buds and simmer them for four to five minutes or make a jasmine green tea and steep it as you would a green tea. If you prefer black tea, you may alternatively buy golden jasmine buds black tea. Here is an easy recipe:

2 tsp. food-grade jasmine flower tea

1 C. hot water

Add the water to any suitable kettle and let it boil first. Put roughly 2 tsp. of jasmine flower tea in a T-Sac or mesh tea strainer to a mug, or just put it in the bottom. Pour the boiling water over the jasmine flowers. Let the jasmine flowers steep for two to four minutes with the cup covered. Strain or remove the flowers and serve the tea warm.

Friday

Red Clover Tea

Red clover is used to treat gout, cancer, whooping cough, and asthma. Red clover extracts are also advertised for osteoporosis, high cholesterol, and menopause symptoms.

1 C. red clover blossoms

2 Tbsp. mint (spearmint or peppermint)

4 C. water

honey to sweeten

Verify that there are no pests by checking the flower. Moreover, confirm that the flowers have not been sprayed. In a suitable kettle, boil the water, then remove from the heat. Add mint and clover flowers to the hot water. Leave this tea for around ten to fifteen minutes to steep—a longer steeping period will cool the water. Strain and pour the prepared tea into the cup. To taste, add honey or sugar. Enjoy!

Tip: You can dry red clover flowers at home and store them for making tea. Every year, I air-dry red clover and store it in plastic containers with tight seals. I use it to make iced tea by combining it with 6 C. of water, two decaffeinated tea bags, the red clover, and mint. Both are very healthy and delicious!

Saturday

Mint Tea

If you have mint in your garden, gather a big batch and start drying it. Plant mint straight away in your garden if it isn't already there. It grows quickly, so you'll have enough to start making tea in a few weeks. Planting mint in its own container or bucket prevents it from encroaching on other plants. You can use fresh and dried mint leaves in this tea because they both have many benefits and a delicious flavor. After steeping for ten minutes, the tea will cool.

Ingredients:

1 lb. mint leaves

Mint leaves should be washed with water, then dried on paper towels. (It's alright to leave a few little stems.) When the mint has completely dried, spread it out on a tablecloth and place it in a dry, dark environment. Leave for up to a week to dry. Crush the leaves and stems into crumbs once dried. Put it into a jar. When serving, add 1 C. of boiling water to 3 to 4 Tbsp. of dry mint. Remove the mint.

Sunday

Lavender Tea

A good way to reenergize yourself on Sundays is to have lavender tea. It works like a miracle again the intestinal problem. According to research, drinking lavender tea can aid with digestive problems like nausea, vomiting, and upset stomach. It may make you feel better. According to several researchers, drinking lavender tea can help your mind relax and reduce anxiety. We cannot guarantee that it will treat all of your ailments. However, there is no disputing how calming a cup of lavender tea is. One teaspoon of dried lavender is enough for one serving, and you can use more to make tea for the family. You can adjust the steeping time based on your personal preferences for the flavor. Here is how you can make it:

1 ¼ C. (10 ounces) boiling water

2 tsp. lavender buds, dried or fresh

1 tsp. honey (or maple syrup or agave syrup)

First, start by boiling the water in any suitable pot or kettle. Put the lavender buds in a tea ball or tea strainer. Place this tea strainer with lavender buds in hot water for five minutes to steep. After removing the tea sieve, add the honey and stir. Enjoy right away!

HEALING TREATMENTS

A potent technique for balancing and restoring your life force energy is aromatherapy. Discover which essential oils can help open, activate, and balance your body's energy centers as you read on to learn how to use them for chakras. Aromatherapy doesn't receive nearly as much attention as sound healing, color therapy, and other well-known chakra healing techniques. You shouldn't undervalue this effective technique, either. If done properly, aromatherapy can be a powerful tool for reviving your energy, calming the mind, and bringing balance and serenity to the energy centers in your body.

Better yet, you might be able to get started right away with supplies you already have at home. What really is aromatherapy, then? The use of pure plant extracts for therapeutic healing is known as aromatherapy. It's a type of holistic healing that encourages your overall health—mind, body, and soul.

Essential Oils for Chakras

Essential oil treatment, which dates back thousands of years, uses natural, usually fragrant chemicals found in a variety of plants for their therapeutic benefits. People have developed ways to include specific plants, herbs, and flowers into their lives ever since learning about their medicinal properties. These methods include adding them to food, using them to make medicines, using them topically for sore spots, and extracting their scent. While many people are already aware that essential oils have nice aromas, each plant also has an energetic resonance that enables it to treat both the physical body and the subtle energy body. Essential oil therapy is fantastic for those of us who think too much since it bypasses our brain processes and resonates with us on a fundamental level. It can assist us in moving from a state of being in which our emotions are overwhelming to one in which we feel more able to breathe and take things slowly. Moreover, it can be used in bodywork to treat particular kinds of pain and reduce muscle tension. Essential oil therapy provides instant access to healing. Furthermore, finding high-quality oils is simple, they are portable, and there are many applications for them (including applying them to the body, diffusing them in your home or office, and making blends and elixirs, among other things).

Root chakra. The purpose of the following essential oils is to keep you grounded and let you reconnect to the earth element. You can use them for massage, inhale them through diffusers, or add a few drops to your bathtub. Buying candles with the aromas of the following oils will also work like magic:

- Cedarwood oil
- Rosemary oil
- Sandalwood oil
- Basil oil
- Patchouli oil
- Black pepper
- Geranium

Sacral chakra. Your sacral chakra can be unblocked by inhaling the aromas of these essential oils.

- Orange oil
- Tangerine oil
- Cinnamon oil
- Bergamot oil
- Neroli oil
- Cypress oil
- Cardamom oil

Use any of the suggested methods from the next section to introduce them into your life.

Solar plexus chakra. Your solar plexus chakra can be best balanced by introducing the below essential oils into your life. You can use a single one or use two to three in a blend. It entirely depends on your personal preference.

- Lemon oil
- Lemongrass oil
- Coriander oil
- Juniper oil
- Lime oil
- Rosemary oil
- Pine oil

Heart chakra. To open your heart chakra, you can use any of the following essential oils. I personally keep my diffuser filled with lavender oil, which is not only therapeutic for my chakra but also gives my living room a great fragrance.

- Lavender oil
- Rose oil
- Jasmine oil
- Geranium oil
- Goldenrod oil
- Cypress oil
- Rosewood oil
- Pine oil

Throat chakra. If you want to work on the health of the throat chakra, then using these essential oils will definitely help:

- Basil oil
- Cypress oil
- Peppermint oil
- Chamomile oil
- Coriander oil
- Juniper oil
- Eucalyptus oil
- Lavender oil

Third eye chakra. Whenever you meditate or do yoga to open your third eye chakra, you can use these essential oils through diffusers for a better experience:

- Frankincense oil
- Basil oil
- Juniper oil
- Rosemary oil
- Lemon oil
- Pine oil
- Cedarwood oil
- Sandalwood oil

Crown chakra. If you want to feel more enlightened and aware, introducing the following essential oils into your life will definitely help:

- Frankincense oil
- Sandalwood oil
- Saffron oil
- Jasmine oil
- Cedarwood oil
- Lavender oil
- Lime oil

Please read all labels and packaging directions before using essential oils. Remember that essential oils are quite concentrated, so before using them, make sure to dilute them by mixing in a neutral oil, like coconut oil. Use secure storage. Moreover, pick products free of synthetic chemicals.

Essential Oil Blends:

Essential oil blends contain two or more oils topical use or aromatherapy to calm the mind, body, and spirit and to alleviate chakra imbalances. Some mixtures that are recommended include:

- A cypress, vetiver, and sandalwood oil blend for the root chakra
- A Ylang, lavender, and jasmine oil blend for the sacral chakra
- A lavender and cardamom oil blend for solar plexus chakra
- A marjoram, lavender, and chamomile oil blend for the heart chakra
- A eucalyptus and sage oil blend for the throat chakra
- Go with a jasmine and myrrh oil blend for third eye chakra
- Try a lotus and myrrh oil blend for the crown chakra

Again, while making these blends, make sure to also add some neutral oil like coconut oil to dilute them. Usually, the bottles of oils come with a dilution formula, so follow that. Otherwise, use two parts of neutral oil and one part of essential oil to dilute them.

How to Use Essential Oils

Essential oils come to mind when we think of aromatherapy, especially given how well-liked they have been over the previous ten years. Essential oils are organic substances that are obtained from a plant's flower, bark, leaves, or fruit. So, where do you start? The intention is the key to releasing the power of aromatherapy and any chakra healing technique. When trying to heal the energy centers in your body, it's essential to have a clear goal in mind. For me, this is taking a deep breath before beginning and stating my goal to myself aloud or silently. Here are a few techniques you may use to use aromatherapy to open, activate, and heal the energy centers in your body.

With a Diffuser.

Select a spot for your diffuser that will keep it close to you all day. Use an oil that is related to the chakra you want to heal, either alone or in a blend. The ability to combine a diffuser with different chakra healing techniques is what I value most. For instance, while my diffuser is running, I can journal, practice meditation, engage in creative endeavors, or work with crystals. For the sacral chakra, which is linked to the element of water, and the heart chakra, which is linked to the element of air, using an essential oil diffuser can be a particularly effective technique. However, this technique is beneficial for all chakras, and using an essential oil diffuser can be a potent approach to calm your inner energy.

Personal Cologne. Using your essential oil as a personal fragrance will allow you to enjoy the therapeutic scent all day long if you're out and about. First, select an essential oil that corresponds to the chakra you want to work on. Then, make sure the essential oil you select is suitable for skin application. Some essential oils shouldn't be used on the skin, such as "hot" oils, because of skin sensitivity and allergies; also, different people may respond to essential oils in different ways. Always follow the usage instructions, and if you have any concerns, speak with a medical expert. Once you've decided on an oil, you can apply it to your chest, neck, forehead, or temples. Using essential oil roll-on bottles is a great choice for this, especially because the majority are pre-diluted, typically with coconut oil, for safety.

Massaging with Essential Oils. Applying essential oil to the chest and throat region may help to repair the throat chakra. You can apply it on your forehead and temples to open your third eye chakra. Moreover, you might apply an essential oil to the soles of your feet for the root chakra because this chakra symbolizes your basis and connection to the soil. Just remember that the same safety precautions I mentioned above also apply here: dilute them for safety.

Add a drop to your drinking water. Please observe all usage and safety guidelines, and make sure your chosen essential oil is suitable for internal use. I know I may sound like a broken record here, but I'll say it again: when done safely, drinking a drop of your preferred essential oil (diluted in water or tea) can be an effective approach to spreading the oil's therapeutic properties throughout the body. Edible essential oils can even be added to herbal teas for more benefits.

Add to your bath. To clear the aura and remove lingering imbalances while calming the mind and soul, add eight to ten drops of the essential oil of your choice to a warm bath. Three times a week, try adding essential oils to the bath water, then meditate to magnify the oils' ability to improve focus and balance.

BOOK4:
DAILY AND SEASONAL RITUALS

What exactly are healing rituals? Well, in simple words, a ritual is any activity or action which is carried out repeatedly to gain certain benefits or produce certain effects. Any activity that is carried out to heal your soul and prana, and to unblock your blocked chakras is a healing ritual. It is imperative to mention here that in different parts of the world, approaches to spiritual healing are different, and people use many different rituals to tap into the energies of the universe and to connect to them. In this book, while I will explain all the different rituals that you can carry out to heal yourself, I will also enlist daily and seasonal rituals that will affect your life positively. The purpose of the rituals shared in this book is to help you spiritually and emotionally cleanse yourself by getting rid of negative energies. I hope you get the best of the experience!

DAILY RITUALS

Daily rituals, in my opinion, are a collection of tasks to complete each day with the aim of being attentive to the moment and how the task makes us feel. Routines can be boring daily duties that are usually executed automatically and involve multitasking. Daily rituals, on the other hand, help to foster a positive mindset and improve our general well-being. The ten simple rituals listed below can be easily incorporated into your daily life. Expose your skin to natural light as soon as you wake up. Better yet, spend some time outside. The sun will help to regulate your circadian rhythm, or sleep/wake cycle, which is a terrific approach to promoting healthy sleeping patterns. It will also naturally elevate your mood and energy levels.

Balancing with Breathing

The health advantages of conscious, deep abdominal breathing are numerous. Reducing the effects of the stress hormone cortisol helps to lower blood pressure and heart rate and helps to induce relaxation. It has been demonstrated that even ten minutes a day of deep breathing is beneficial for health, particularly for reducing anxiety.

Multitaskers will definitely love this: why not do some deep breathing exercises outside in the sunshine as soon as you wake up? Whether you are waiting to meet someone at the office, sitting at home in your pajamas, or taking a work break at your desk, you can start where you are. Consider your head floating over the tip of your tailbone as you find the most comfortable natural position for your spine. Pay attention to your breathing. Close your eyes if you'd like, or just avert your attention. We don't want the boss to think you're dozing off at work. Imagine as you breathe that the energy inside you is moving upward from the tailbone along the spine and right up to the top of the head. The energy moves back down toward the tailbone as you exhale. Inhale slowly for at least 3 breaths this way. Then, we'll start balancing each chakra from its base to its top.

Breathe to be rooted. While breathing deeply, follow these steps The feet should be firmly planted on the ground. Allow the hands to rest palms down on the thighs. Imagine the tip of your tailbone as a source of crimson energy that flows forth and downward. As you silently repeat this mantra, "I am anchored," take three deep breaths.

Enhance creativity with breathing. While breathing deeply, follow these steps: A few times, gently rock the belly and low back forward and backward. Keep the hands near the lower abdomen between the navel and the pubic bone. Imagine the sacrum, hips, and low belly radiating orange energy. As you silently say this affirmation: "I am present," take three deep breaths. Gently twist the spine a few times in either direction.

Be mindful. While breathing deeply, follow these steps: At the waist, place the hands for support. Imagine a flow of yellow energy from the upper belly to the navel, then out to the sides of the body and around to the middle of the back. As you silently repeat to yourself: "I am centered," take three slow breaths.

Open Your Heart by Breathing. While breathing deeply follow these steps: Roll your shoulders up toward your ears, back, and down, first in one then in both directions. Bring your palms together at the center of the chest with the thumbs resting on the body. Imagine a green energy field around your heart, chest, and upper back from the front, sides, and rear. As you silently repeat this mantra, "I am balanced," take three deep breaths.

Purify your energies. While breathing deeply, follow these steps: Roll your head slowly and softly in either half or full circles to activate the Visshudha chakra. Allow hands to rest anywhere on the body by touching the center finger to the thumb. Imagine a line of light blue energy running from the top of your shoulders to your ears. As you silently repeat this mantra, "I am peaceful," take three deep breaths.

Activate the inner eye. While breathing deeply, follow these steps: If you can, close your eyes and concentrate on the area between your brows for the inner eye, or Ajna. Bring the thumbs to the inner brow, where the eye meets the bridge of your nose, while holding the palms together. Allowing the head to rest lightly on the thumbs will produce minimal pressure. Imagine a deep blue energy field surrounding the base of the skull and extending from the forehead. Repeat this mantra silently to yourself three times: "I am clear."

Induce awareness. While breathing deeply, follow these steps: Sahasrara, the crown chakra, invites awareness to the top of the head and the area immediately above it. Anywhere on the body, rest the hands with the palms up and join the tip of the index finger to the thumb. Imagine violet energy coming from the crest of the head and rising upward. As you silently say this affirmation: "I am linked," take three deep breaths.

Continue the breathing practice by taking three breaths up and down the spine after you are completed. Go about the rest of your day and perhaps even change out of your pajamas after taking note of how you are feeling physically, mentally, and spiritually. (Or not!)

Aura Cleansing Bath

Have you ever had a mind-straining conversation with someone then experienced a strange feeling that something wasn't quite right or that made you uncomfortable? What about those interactions where you merely leave feeling exhausted? What about the interactions or events that inspire you and make you feel energized? Or when a person enters a room, and everyone sees them as they do? These are the vibrational frequencies that we are continuously emitting as a species.

Every day, we come into contact with a wide variety of people, circumstances, and events; as a result, we are continually picking up subtle energies from these exchanges, both direct and indirect. In addition to that, our words, emotions, and thoughts all carry EMFs of their own. The ambient energies that we come into contact with impact our own energy field because it is continually absorbing and emitting vibrations. However, occasionally, the negative energies we come into contact with might persist and build up over time. Fortunately, our energy body is continually readjusting itself to bring us back into balance. With a nice aromatic bath, you can literally wash off those energies—but it has to be a spiritual bath to get rid of them.

A "spiritual bath" vs. a regular bath. If you're anything like me, bathing isn't something you naturally want to do. Showers are my favorite and preferred method of personal hygiene. When I take contemplative showers, I also make a point of clearing my energy as the water flows over me and down the drain. Even without the extra intention, regular bathing or showering for physical hygiene does induce relaxation and advance general well-being. However, spiritual baths are very different. They serve as a practice for spiritual hygiene to refresh your delicate senses and cleanse your own energy body. A spiritual bath can help you feel more refreshed, renewed, and at peace with yourself. Give yourself twenty to sixty minutes of uninterrupted time to practice this technique.

Steps for Spiritual Bathing

Imagine a spiritual bath as one that revitalizes both your body and soul. We can all relate to the fact that you feel one way before taking a bath and another when you come out. Beyond just the physical body, the mind and spirit are also cleansed in this manner. If there is a "purpose," it is something you and your intention decide. To be present with yourself and your body so that you can work with the internal and energetic healing that arises in that space, however, could be said to be the general objective. And that is where the advantage is. All life intuitively understands that cleaning is therapeutic, calming, and inspirational; perhaps this is one of the reasons why all life needs water.

Depending on your goals, ritual bathing can be approached in a variety of ways. Here are some ideas for intentionally enriching your bath (or shower or foot soak):

Set the space. Always begin in a tidy environment. Make space for the items you want to be surrounded by while organizing your counters and cleaning your tub. Anything you use in this exercise, such as plants, crystals, or candles, should be carefully chosen to evoke the feeling of the energy cleanse you're trying to achieve.

Select the essential oils. When taking a spiritual bath, decide what aroma you want to fill the air. You can do this by burning incense, dripping candles, or diffusing essential oils. It completely depends on you; just make sure it's an aroma that you enjoy or is connected to the emotions you want to experience.

Decide which sound to play. I love using binaural beats or other soothing frequencies, such as music, when I'm bathing. Avoid songs with lyrics and instead listen to instrumental music, such as piano, wind instruments, singing bowls, acoustic guitars, etc. You can add or remove anything from what has previously been discussed; trust your instincts. Choose something that calms you when you hear it and set the volume to a comfortable and quiet level.

Things to use for spiritual cleanse. When setting your environment, keep in mind what makes you feel good. Use sage and palo santo at any time during the procedure. Warm water should be added to the tub for your comfort.

- Natural salt is one of the most effective chemicals for clearing any form of stuck-on negativity from your energies. The best salts are readily available and include pink Himalayan salt, natural sea salt, and Epsom salt. Never use conventional table salt since it contains anti-caking chemicals and has been refined, removing many of the helpful minerals. Use no more than a few good handfuls.
- A baking soda solution can be used. It is a mixture of sodium ions and bicarbonate that is beneficial for bathing, both physically and energetically. Use one-quarter to two cups.
- Lavender has a relaxing impact on your mental and emotional state and can be used to encourage relaxation by boiling whole buds in water or essential oils. Use just enough to create a light scent.

Other things for spiritual bathing.

- Fresh pink and red carnations are simmered in water with honey and coconut milk then drained to preserve the liquid as bath components. It is stated that this assists in easing a shattered heart.
- Fresh red or pink rose petals should be boiled until the color is completely gone. To improve your mood and practice self-love, let it cool and add it to a warm bath. To increase the aroma of your bath, feel free to add additional petals, either fresh or dried.
- There are many different herbs that have been used as a plant medicine for a long time.
- You may find ready-made spiritual bath sets online if you don't have the time to prepare your components. You can just add the mixture to the bathtub per the package instructions and draw a nice bath for yourself accordingly.

Sound Bath

There are other types of baths that can be beneficial for your health besides a soothing soak in the tub. The effects of stress, exhaustion, and despair may be reduced by waves of calming, resonant sound produced by conventional wind and percussion instruments, commonly referred to as a "sound bath." Considering that stress has been linked to diseases like diabetes and heart disease, taking sound baths can be a smart preventive measure to lower your risk of developing chronic illnesses as well. Although there hasn't been much research on this topic, some studies have found that, among other things, taking a sound bath may help you feel better and relieve physical strain.

Gong bath. Gong baths let you "bathe" in the soothing vibrations of sound as a form of passive meditation. Ancient societies have long used sound to promote health; early Egyptian, Greek, and Roman records document the use of gongs. Sessions of gong bathing can be done alone or with others and typically last forty-five minutes to two hours. Participants often lie down and make themselves comfortable with pillows and blankets before a gong bath. Then a facilitator uses a mallet to strike the gong, a percussion instrument in the form of a disc.

How to create a gong bath at home. If you don't want to spend tens or hundreds of dollars to find and book a gong bath session in your area, then don't worry—a calming, unwinding gong bath can be easily made at home. But for that, you will need to follow these few steps:

Set the mood. Create a peaceful environment and soothing location first. Close the windows and doors in a room where you won't be bothered. By drawing the curtains, dimming the lights, or lighting candles, you can create a dim or low-lit environment. Consider using an essential oil diffuser or lighting some calming incense.

Chillax. You might like to lie down on a yoga mat on the ground, on your bed, or on your couch. Try putting a soft pillow under your knees for lower back support or under your head for comfort. Adding more darkness using an eye cushion can help you feel more relaxed. If you don't have one, think about covering your eyes with a scarf. Go for relaxed attire such as leggings, loungewear, or even pajamas. Wear socks or a snug hoodie to be warm and comfortable. Set up your headphones or speakers so you can hear the sound, then listen to the recorded or live gong session you want to quiet the mind

Lie down. Once everything is set up, lie down with your eyes closed and a blanket over you. Beginning with a breathing exercise will help you focus, ground your body, and get the most rewards. Try alternative nostril breathing or the equal breath pattern, for instance. The regulated breathing should then be let go of, and you should just unwind into the sound.

Acupressure

A long-used technique in traditional Chinese medicine is acupressure. Because the notion is based on pressure points and invisible energy lines in your body, it can appear mysterious. The same basic principles apply to acupuncture and acupressure. Acupressure, however, does not employ needles. Applying pressure to certain body locations is known as acupressure, and it is used to treat symptoms like body pain and digestive problems. Self-acupressure can be performed with just your fingertips. Some forms of massage therapy, such as the Japanese technique known as shiatsu, use it. It can also be done as part of acupuncture therapy.

According to traditional Chinese medicine, a healthy body must have a consistent flow of "qi." The best way to describe qi is as life energy that flows through our energy centers or channels. Pressure points are locations along these energy pathways that can facilitate the qi unfettered flow. They are also known as acupoints. The same pressure points are used by acupuncturists, but needles are used to access them. Simply pressing or massaging the point location is all that is required for acupressure.

Steps for acupressure. Acupressure has the advantage of being able to be self-applied. It can be used to cover an entire area, such as the foot or hand, or it can be administered to individual acupoints. The following diagram shows some acupressure points on a hand that can be pressed to heal your prana.

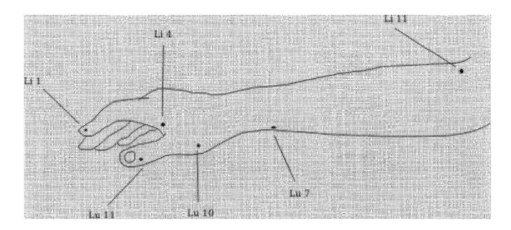

Apply deep, continuous pressure to the acupoint with your thumb or index finger. For one to two minutes, use a circular or up-and-down motion to massage the point. You can apply acupressure as often as you desire.

I would recommend you always see a licensed acupuncturist who has received training in acupressure if you wish to use acupressure to treat a particular problem. And while applying acupressure on yourself, make sure you are in a secure location. When engaging in any activity that could endanger your safety, avoid using acupressure. Acupressure should not be used while driving, for instance.

Daily Dose of Affirmations

Affirmations offer a potent alchemical synthesis of intention, spoken word, and mindfulness to make use of the power or energies of the present moment. Our energy field, also referred to as our physical and nonphysical bodies, is controlled by the energy that flows through it. Our chakras, or energy centers, are contained inside this field of energy. These centers use the mind-body connection to receive and send data and experiences. You can improve your body's energy flow by using affirmations.

What does the science say? Affirmations, do they really work? According to some studies, the answer is yes. According to a study published in 2015, self-affirmation modifies the brain's reaction to health messages and thus causes behavioral change. A 2009 research article, however, concluded that not everyone would benefit from affirmations. Researchers discovered that repeating a positive self-statement made those with low self-esteem feel worse than those who didn't. On the other hand, participants with high self-esteem felt marginally better than those who didn't repeat the sentence. The only way you will know if affirmations may be effective for you is to try them out for yourself. Saying positive words of affirmation definitely has a balancing effect on our chakras

Chakra affirmations: how to use them? Chakra affirmations can be incorporated into your life in a variety of ways. You can add them to prayers, listen to a recording, or include them in your meditation routine. But don't anticipate trumpeting angels and separating clouds. Adora Winquist, self-defined modern alchemist and vibrational medicine expert, states that sometimes the changes are subtle. She advises writing your affirmations and reactions to them in a journal. There are times when you'll see yourself reacting to someone or something in a better way.

Affirmations for the root chakra. You can say the following words to yourself to heal or balance your root chakra.

- I am a vibrant and healthy person.
- I am safely and deeply connected to the Earth and my body.
- I can feel the ground firmly beneath my feet.
- I truly honor the temple of my body with reverence and deep care.
- I am always open to life's new opportunities.
- I am fully committed to fulfilling my life's purpose.

Affirmations for sacral chakra. You can say the following words to yourself to heal or balance your sacral chakra.

- I truly accept the flow of life.
- I will use my energy for creative expression.
- I feel free to express my emotions in a healthy way.
- I really honor my sensual expression.
- I am an empowered sexual being.
- My creativity flows effortlessly.

Affirmations for solar plexus chakra. You can say the following words to yourself to heal or balance your solar plexus chakra.

- I am a decisive being.
- I can make clear and definitive choices.
- I can take healthy risks.
- I truly commit to my direction in life.
- I am always open to new possibilities in life.
- I feel empowered to live my best life.

Affirmations for heart chakra. You can say the following words to yourself to heal or balance your heart chakra.

- I keep my heart open to sharing, giving, and receiving love.
- I feel more compassion for myself and others
- I am nothing but a conduit for love and peace.
- I am filled with gratitude for my ability to love.
- My heart is filled with unconditional love for all other beings.

Affirmations for throat chakra. You can say the following words to yourself to heal or balance your throat chakra.

- I am listening to my own inner knowing.
- I only speak my truth.
- I will let my voice be heard.
- I truly trust my conviction and act on my reality.
- I intend no harm with my words.
- I speak with conviction, grace, authenticity, and courage.
- I love to express my creativity.

Affirmations for third eye chakra. You can say the following words to yourself to heal or balance your third eye chakra.

- I can clearly see my life's purpose.
- I feel connected to the spiritual world.
- I feel open to the truths of the universe.
- I feel connected to the divine power within.

Affirmations for crown chakra. You can say the following words to yourself to heal or balance your crown chakra.

- I am experiencing unity with all things.
- I want to surrender myself to the divine.
- I want to align with the highest aspect of my being.
- I can feel the divine light and love flow through me.

Rituals Before Bedtime

Sleep is the body's natural way to heal itself; while physical body cells heal during sleep, you can also use this time to heal your chakras. Here is what you really need to do before going to bed.

- Inhale deeply for five deep breaths and exhale through your mouth.
- Visualize a lovely light encircling you in all directions and on all sides of your body. I usually imagine a purple light. You will begin to feel this bubble or cocoon of light traveling through your body as soon as you become aware of it. Starting at the top of your head, feel it illuminating every single one of your body's cells, tissues, organs, and fibers all the way to your feet.
- Visualize yourself releasing your energy from negative people, environments, and circumstances. Think of all the things that throughout the day caused you to feel pressured, nervous, unhappy, helpless, or furious as fishhooks that are releasing.
- Wash your energy in the lovely healing light that surrounds and flows through you as you feel it returning to you. This light cleanses the heavy energy from your body, mind, and soul by acting as an "energetic vehicle wash."
- Send a different hue of light (I usually select white) through your body when you feel your energy readjust. From the top of your head crown to your toes, feel this energy flowing down. See how your energy field is being strengthened by this final light show.

This regular activity will refocus your energy at night and make you blissful. This bedtime ritual will not only induce deep and peaceful sleep but also helps to realign your chakras. You will get up next feeling more energized.

CRYSTALS

Crystals are used to empower the strengths connected to a specific stone as well as to draw forth or divert energy. They are also employed for healing and rebalancing. Working with crystals and stones enables us to connect with the inherent energy of the earth to nurture our talents and strengths. Moreover, it enables us to access our talents, get in touch with our gifts, get back in balance, heal, and raise our consciousness. Crystals or stones can be used in a variety of different ways to solve spiritual problems.

Crystals can be used in a wide variety of ways. One typical method is to carry a little crystal in your pocket or wear it as a necklace, pair of earrings, or bracelet. When you wear a crystal, its energetic frequency stays in resonance with you all day. Another approach to using stones, particularly while performing chakra healing, is to lie down in a comfortable position, place chakra-specific crystals on each individual chakra, and then allow yourself to meditate or simply clear your mind while the stones magnify the job you're already doing—whether it be breaking patterns, growing your gifts, opening a particular chakra, letting go of something, or striving toward a different objective. Holding crystals in your left (receiving) hand while meditating allows you to absorb the crystal's healing energies. This is an excellent additional technique to use crystals.

What Are Crystals Used For?

In order to keep our chakras and energies in balance, we occasionally need to rely on tools. Crystals are a very potent energy source and healer. It takes an enormous amount of energy—millions of years' worth of heat and pressure, in fact—to form a single crystal. Crystals communicate with our own energy field to affect and sway us. Based on their own special characteristics, they absorb our energy and reflect it. The chakras and crystals are energetic partners that help us connect to the larger energy field and find our place there.

We can tune into the well-being and vibrancy of the chakras and realign them using instruments like gemstones. Working with crystals and the chakras reveals how intricately related we are to everything in our environment. We can learn vital information about our personal energies from them, including how we are reflecting and refracting stories about our own experiences into the outside world.

Each crystal has a distinct vibration and function of its own. You align yourself with the vibration of that stone by selecting it to assist you with a particular objective or by allowing yourself to be pulled to one crystal in particular because it interacts with your energy body directly (and often benefits the physical body as well). Rose quartz, for instance, not only supports the heart chakra but also lowers blood pressure. It is all connected. There are numerous ways to invoke the healing energies of crystals, and there is no one method that works for all precious stones. Whether you wish to use crystals to align chakras, manifest intentions, help the body heal and harmonize, or balance your emotions, your journey is entirely unique to you. Every single crystal is completely different and has its own healing qualities; in fact, the healing power of a crystal can be influenced by its color. Moreover, different crystal forms will have varying strengths and abilities, and how you use your crystals is also important. Let's examine some of the various ways in which individuals are compelled to use healing gemstones.

Intention. You can employ the healing energy of specific crystals to strengthen and realize your wishes by calling on their particular strengths. Aims or goals that you have for your life are called intentions. To increase your confidence, this could mean anything from yearning for deeper connections to wanting more money and prosperity or better mental health. It could also mean yearning for connection or self-forgiveness. It might be a desire to let go of past hurts and embark on a new beginning, or it might be a desire to improve focus in order to realize a dream. By selecting gems that support your goals, you can attract the force necessary to change and reshape reality.

Realigning the chakras. Using the healing vibrations of crystals can assist in removing obstructions and shaking away stale energy from these spinning discs of energy. Since each chakra is associated with a specific color, you can typically determine which chakra a particular crystal is energetically connected to by looking at the stone's color. The root chakra is red, the solar plexus chakra is yellow, the sacral chakra is orange, the throat chakra is blue, the heart chakra is green, the third eye chakra is purple, and the crown chakra is purple.

Physical conditions. Crystals can be used for physical, mental, and spiritual healing. Some crystals may be able to relieve bodily ills and health problems. The high vibrations of the stones may be able to shake off energetic blockages in the body that may be aggravating certain health concerns. Some healing gemstones also possess deeply calming energy that can aid in reducing the symptoms of stress and worry, many of which can manifest in the body and impair the immune system. For instance, amethyst is a wonderful stone for reducing headaches and promoting sleep. Citrine's good energy can increase your energy levels. Aventurine can be used to hasten your recovery from an illness, while bloodstones can support good circulation.

Emotional and psychological support. The fact that crystals may provide a great deal of emotional and psychological support is another incredibly common reason why people pick them. Healing gemstones can help you access suppressed emotions and can calm ruffled nerves. Moreover, they can help you manage strong emotions and keep you from feeling overpowered. Again, different gems offer unique abilities when it comes to supporting and balancing emotions. For instance, rose quartz is an excellent gem for enhancing your sense of self-care, mending past hurts, and widening your heart. Amethyst relaxes the mind, clear quartz can aid in bringing clarity and insight, and moonstone balances strong hormonal activity.

How do Crystals Heal?

Crystals have long been thought of as having power. Crystals, regardless of size, exude a sense of power and mystery. Using crystals and chakra energy in a positive way might help you reactivate your individual essence. You may embody your actual, honest self via a crystal and become closer to finding the physical, mental, and emotional balance you're looking for in your life. It's crucial to keep in mind that each individual's experience of working with crystals and chakras will be unique. Your level of awareness is the only element that matters. Whether you decide to meditate, work with crystals, or do both at once, balancing your chakras will enable you to live your life to the fullest, most expanded manifestation of who you are.

Placing a crystal on an appropriate chakra for roughly fifteen minutes to rebalance the energy center is one technique to access a crystal's therapeutic ability. Feel the vibrations entering your being as you hold the crystal in your hands. Say, "I am using this crystal and dedicate it to my highest good and the good of all others," while focusing your concentration on the crystal. I request that it be given power right away so that it can cooperate with my own goals. Use high-vibration crystals to amplify your consciousness. Either sit with the crystal in your hand or keep it on your third eye or crown chakra. Gently inhale and concentrate your attention on the stone. Allow the process to take its course without attempting to see or feel anything.

Ways to Use Crystals

The most prevalent connection between crystals and chakras is through vibration, resetting, and opening the chakras by working with crystal energy's vibratory strength. The power of crystals can be used on a regular basis to cleanse and re-energize your chakras, which helps you keep your energy at its peak and increases your sense of personal power. Each chakra is associated with a different gemstone and using a crystal as an energy source during activities like meditation is immensely cleansing. Select a crystal that is known to have attributes similar to the chakra you are focusing on and take a moment to attune to the crystal for a well-balanced crystal healing or meditation.

Place on the body. Placing crystals on specific areas of your body is a procedure that is popular among individuals who specialize in crystal treatment (but is equally simple to perform at home). This technique typically works in harmony with the chakras; for instance, if the heart chakra is blocked, you can place a heart chakra crystal, such as rose quartz, nearby and allow the soothing vibrations to permeate and calm the spirit.

Wear. Using the energies of gemstone jewelry is among the best methods to bring crystal healing into your life. Having the stone pushed against the skin allows healing vibrations to communicate with your body and regulate your chakras, whether you choose crystal bead bracelets, necklaces, or even rings. Another low-maintenance technique to maximize crystal healing is by wearing gemstone jewelry.

Pendulum. Another method of healing that works well for the practice of divination is the use of crystal pendulums. Your crystal-weighted pendulum serves as a conduit for the cosmos to send you advice. The pendulum also aids in clearing out bad energy from a space and pointing out where solutions are required to assist with healing choices.

Treating particular maladies. You can also use a specific crystal layout if you want to focus on a particular area of healing. As with any spiritual and emotional healing, desire is everything in this technique to get the energy flowing along the highways of your body. You can choose to align the chakras with the seven-crystal arrangement, and you can channel energy coming in or going out by turning the crystals, so they are facing inward or outward.

Keep them with you in your pocket or bag. Keeping a crystal close by helps you live more in harmony with its energy and raises your awareness of your healing process and overall health. When you need an instant boost of energy or a minute of meditation, take out your favorite crystals and hold them in your hands.

Clear grid. You can supercharge your healing stones to increase their potency by arranging your crystals in a grid-like design. Cleanse and refresh your jewels, smudge the space, and arrange your crystals in a grid pattern. To assist you in mapping out the magic, pick a grid fabric if you are new to the practice.

Put in your bathtub. Run a goddess bath for yourself—add your hot water and happy crystals, then get in there. A crystal bath is a wonderful approach to receiving a miraculous boost of healing and detoxification. We tend to be gentler, less stressed, and more receptive to the crystals' gifts when submerged in warm water. For this, selenite is a gentle angelic stone.

Place them across in surroundings.

Simply having crystals around you will infuse your surroundings with positive energy, provide protection and self-love, and keep out negative energy. Whether you need some healing in your bedroom or your office or when communicating carefully, include crystals in your décor to instantly change the vibe. Black tourmaline is an incredible stone for protection against electromagnetic frequencies (EMF) in the workplace.

How to Choose Your Stone?

There is a vast array of therapeutic gemstones and crystals available. Knowing which stone you wish to invite into your environment can seem intimidating. The reminder to tune in, listen to our own intuition, and have faith in our own wisdom is one of the most crucial teachings crystals impart to us. In the same way that everything in the cosmos is composed of energy, so are our bodies, mind, and soul. We can listen to the signals and messages the planet is trying to send us if we can access that power.

Assessing the crystals you are drawn to (or which ones are drawn to you) will help you find the ideal one. When you read about a crystal, see a picture of it, or hear its name, you can sense a pull inside that draws you to that particular stone. Each crystal also has its own unique set of therapeutic qualities. We can choose healing stones based on their distinct characteristics to aid us in our decision-making because occasionally we are not aware of our own strengths and shortcomings. Using the zodiac as a guide to crystal selection is another option.

Knowing which zodiac signs correspond to which crystals might help you find a collection of stones that resonate with the stars.

The Shape of the Crystal

The healing stone's strength and how it affects you can vary depending on the crystal's shape, which also carries its own entrancing energy.

- Point: A point is useful for focusing energy and is usually used for manifestation.
- Sphere: A sphere provides full harmonic energy from all directions.
- Cube: A cube provides stable grounding energy that promotes balance and peace.
- Apex: the apex of a pyramid, which connects the earth to heaven, senses energy rising.
- Tumbled stones: stones are simple to carry as talismans or apply to chakras.

Crystals for Root Chakra

Garnet

Garnet is a stone of splendor, a brilliant ruby red with splashes of spirit. Allows your heart chakra to open up, warm your soul, and reclaim the vitality that can wane with time. The best uses include developing creative abilities, boosting metabolism, removing toxins, giving strength in trying circumstances, and cultivating balanced energy.

Hematite

The silvery grace of hematite, which resembles a falling star and bestows upon you the gift of inner strength and confidence, is a strong and potent crystal that can protect you from negative energy and assist you in extending your safety limits. Best for: blood circulation, willpower, courage, mental acuity, and intuition

Obsidian

Obsidian is a raw, valuable stone formed from the lava of a volcano, and it is always prepared to offer its curative protection to anybody who wears it. It's one of the best shields you could have, whether it's for everyday use or in trying circumstances. The best application is for: blocking out bad energy. It is actually believed that obsidian will absorb it and even stop things like psychic attacks. When faced with challenging circumstances, use this stone.

Jasper

Known for enhancing your ability to feel more deeply and see farther, this stone has long been worn by shamans, high priests, and kings. Jasper is also always prepared to assist you while you fly high while also keeping your feet on the ground. Best used for: dispelling harmful or negative thoughts, fostering tranquility, increasing focus, and relieving tension. It is believed to provide emotional support, increase self-control, and encourage grounding energies.

Bloodstone

Bloodstone was purported to contain the blood from Christ's tears back in the Middle Ages. Bloodstone is a stunning healer recognized for its capacity to increase circulation and raise your self-esteem, regardless of whichever spiritual side you represent. Bloodstone is usually used to treat blood conditions like anemia and poor circulation, as its name suggests. It is employed as an aphrodisiac in India. Excellent for intuition and self-esteem as well.

Carnelian

The bright light of carnelian will ignite your libido and help you overcome your personal obstacles. Carnelian, a magnificent sacral and root chakra strengthener, encourages you to accelerate. Best used for: boosting metabolism, assisting menopause, and enhancing focus. It is excellent for balancing the sacral chakra because of its crimson hue. The fear of dying is lessened by the carnelian, which was also supposed to safeguard the deceased on their trip through the afterlife.

Black Tourmaline

Black tourmaline is incredibly grounding. It has tremendous strength to clear toxic vibrations and restore purity to the body, mind, and soul, and acts as a shield against the harmful effects of electromagnetic fields. Best used for: staying grounded, decision-making, protection from negative energy, as well as lowering anxiety and depressive symptoms.

Tiger's Eye

Tiger's eye is a wonderful stone for cutting through self-doubt so you can make decisions from a position of clarity. It is the golden stone that frees the body and mind from the chains of anxiety. Best for fostering courage, concentration, prosperity, and defense

Smoky Quartz

With exquisite smoky quartz, let the soft fog of relaxation penetrate into every crevice of your spirit. Smoky quartz, a magnificent grounding stone, is renowned for its capacity to neutralize any tension and keep you both soft and strong at the same time. Best for: grounding, boosting good vibes, blocking electromagnetic fields, and balancing the root chakra

Black Onyx

Black onyx, another of the bodyguard's black stones, will help you in healing your base root chakra and in maintaining your composure. Similar to obsidian, this black rock promotes the flow of both physical and mental strength. It promotes the development of your inner warrior and keeps you grounded so you can channel that energy into every strand of your being. When we once again feel confident, strong, and whole, we can be courageous in our passions and creativity. Without getting concerned that someone else will take it over, we are free to occupy as much space as we need and sit in our own soul's seat.

Moss Agate

Although the heart chakra is moss agate's primary chakra of affinity, the root chakra can also benefit from the stone's earthy vitality. The worry and miseries that are weighing you down can be washed away by this stone, which is pure spring rain. Farmers usually employed moss agate, which radiates with Gaia energy, to produce a plentiful harvest. It's an excellent gem to have close and use for root chakra treatment because it promotes abundance. The elements of water, stone, woodland, and shade are all present in moss agate. It calms agitated minds and raging hearts. It makes your immune system perform excellently and guarantees that you can experience serenity in all of its fullness since you feel secure and sacred in your body.

Crystals for Solar Plexus

Pyrite

One of the strongest shields to use against electromagnetic fields and other types of negative attacks is pyrite, a stone so powerful it ignites. This is the Achilles of the crystal world, brimming with manly force. Best used for: cleaning the lower chakras, removing negative thought patterns, boosting confidence, especially in leadership situations, and defense against negative energy and psychic attacks.

Citrine

Citrine exudes health, riches, and the ability to shed bad energy. It is sunny brilliant, and eager to awaken you from sleep. This stone cannot contain negative energy, serving as a stark reminder to take the good with the bad. The best applications include grounding bad energy, assisting in the resolution of interpersonal or group conflicts, encouraging love and happiness, and protecting against people who would hurt your feelings as an emotional defense against resentment and envy.

Calcite

Calcite is a treasure of crystalline limestone that is brimming with vibrant vitamin D. Get a dose of positive energy when you use this stone to enhance your sexual and creative abilities. The best applications are boosting motivation and energy, developing emotional intelligence, using positive thinking, and magnifying energy.

Golden Mookaite

Mookaite's golden hue has a special resonance with the solar plexus. There is only one site on Earth where Mookaite can be found, and that is along the Mooka River in Western Australia. Its close ties to the electromagnetic current of the Earth have helped it gain popularity. It has stimulating effects and is said to be antiaging. The solar plexus is especially sensitive to the golden hue.

Crystals for Heart Chakra

Rose Quartz

It is for people who are prepared to reestablish trust, peace, and unconditional love within their inner world. Rose quartz is perfect in pink and offers deep sweet healing to the heart chakra. The best applications include mending emotional wounds, developing heavenly love, and enhancing friendships and compassion.

Jade

Jade, known as the "guru of good luck," is a wonderful addition to your feng shui and is a symbol of bringing wealth and prosperity. Jade's soothing touch is filled with joy and harmony, making it a must for everyone who wants good things to come their way. Best used for: preventing disease, letting go of unfavorable thoughts, and fostering peaceful relationships.

Malachite

Malachite, which is stunning in green, is a favored stone for the heart chakra. Get assistance severing unhealthy connections, improve your resistance to electromagnetic fields, experiencing luck and prosperity in both work and pleasure, and strengthening the immune system, traveling, treating motion sickness, and vertigo.

Aventurine

Aventurine is incredible when it comes to attracting good luck and bringing flawless wealth into your life. It acts as an amplifier of all the luck in the world. It also balances the physical, emotional, and spiritual aspects of being because of its connection to the heart chakra. The best applications include fostering leadership traits, accepting change, and boosting creative inspiration. Helps with healing for people with heart disease, circulation issues, and those who are recovering from surgery or sickness.

Opal

The opal is a sight to behold, with the brilliance of a pearl atop rainbow flames. This full spectrum stone of healing is well known for spreading loving, possessing upbeat energy and illuminating your aura. Best for: invoking independent thought, removing negative energy, fostering creativity, and raising cosmic consciousness

Amazonite

The amazonite courage stone encourages you to tap into your inner fortitude so you can live fully while not draining your emotional essence. This stone is excellent for releasing traumas that may become immobilized in the body and returning you to a state of sound harmony. Best suited for: healing trauma, combating self-destructive behavior and gaining self-confidence

Unakite

A composite of red jasper and epidote stones that perfectly complement one another and represent solid cooperative connections. The interlacing colors of this bridal gift represent growing together.

Green Calcite

Green calcite is renewing and refreshing, calming the eye and clearing the heart of accumulated emotion. It brings the heart chakra back into balance, allowing energy and emotions to flow and healing old wounds. We may attract the kind of love we want into our lives by using green calcite to help us articulate our desires.

Mangano Calcite/Pink Calcite

Shades of pink calcite purify and bring harmony to the heart chakra, similarly to green calcite. Pink calcite promotes laughing, a deeper spiritual understanding of love, and empathy. It fosters kinship and encourages joy and laughing.

Crystals for Third Eye

Stone Celestite

Celestite is a relaxing stone with strong vibrations that is claimed to be linked to spiritual worlds. This delicate crystal, one of the angel stones, is used for contemplative meditation and attracts universal wisdom. High vibrations, letting go of resentment and negativity, connecting with the spirit worlds, cultivating inner compassion, and accessing limitless wisdom are the best uses for these energies.

Amethyst

Amethyst is one of the holiest and most spiritual healing stones due to its purple colors and strong defensive abilities. A fantastic meditation tool designed for people who desire to reach new heights. Best for: preventing fear and guilt, promoting serenity, reducing anxiety, and producing happy dreams.

Labradorite

It is a stone of amazing change that works best for chakra balancing, aura protection, and banishing depressed energy from your life. Use this sparkling stone of starlight to plunge into profound awareness. When you need to alter and find your inner courage, use this. It is also a fantastic communicator, motivator, and aid for people seeking deeper meaning in life.

Fluorite

Fluorite extends an invitation to those who have trouble making decisions to come down from the fence. The worldly guidance provided by this stone is renowned for guaranteeing that the heart and the mind may live in harmony. The best usage for it is to calm a disturbed mind. This is such an excellent stone for figuring out your life's path, which is usually disregarded in the daily commotion. Excellent for awakening the third eye as well.

Arfvedsonite

Arfvedsonite is a stunning black crystal with blue and, sometimes, green, gold, and purple light flashes. Arfvedsonite is a powerful and necessary crystal that is used by healers, psychics, and people who want to strengthen their ties to the afterlife. Arfvedsonite is considered to help in developing psychic talents and foresight.

Iolite

The third eye chakra is associated with the lyrical stone Iolite, which is all about bringing forth your inner strength and letting you become the leader you always wanted to be. The three things that it works best for are: kicking bad habits, fostering independence, and promoting new, healthier ways of thinking for the body, mind, and soul.

Topaz

The glimmering topaz gemstone is filled with love and affection. With the help of this higher living stone, you may control your temper, eliminate all traces of poison from your life, and reduce fever. Best used for: clearing migraines, maintaining inner equilibrium preventing overload, enhancing focus, and opening the throat chakra for unobstructed communication.

Crystals for Sacral Chakra

Peach Aventurine

This stone has been dubbed the "Whisper Stone" because it soothes the inner critic. It serves as a reminder that we should feel free to indulge in life's joys.

Citrus Calcite

All forms of calcite have reviving energy and purifying qualities. The solar plexus and sacral chakras are said to benefit, especially from the energetic properties of orange calcite. All forms of calcite have reviving energy and purifying qualities. The solar plexus and sacral chakras are said to benefit, especially from the energetic properties of orange calcite.

Carnelian

The intense orange hue that the ancient Egyptians dubbed "Carnelian" probably served as inspiration for the sun's descent. They connected this stone to the mother goddess's fertility. The gemstone carnelian represents passion, love, and desire.

Snowflake Obsidian

Obsidian is made of lava that underwent a rapid cooling process. Snowflake obsidian is the ideal stone to help us remember to maintain our equilibrium and sense of grounding in the midst of the sacral chakra's intense stimulation.

Sunstone

For the sacral chakra, sunstone is a potent healer. There is a part of us that yearns for the fulfillment of life's small pleasures. Sunstone has a strong connection to the Sun's life force, which gives us energy and encourages action. Moreover, sunstone strengthens our love of the outdoors, which connects with the base chakra.

Crystals for Throat Chakra

Sodalite

Sodalite, also known as the Poets Stone, has the energy of a crashing wave that is overflowing with creativity. Boost your communication, speak your greatest truth, and allow inner calm and reasoning to open the door to a life that shines. Used most effectively for courage, insight, and peaceful connections with loved ones.

Chrysocolla

Deep insight and personal honesty are at the core of the tranquil Chrysocolla. This stone can be useful for people who wish to raise their voices, explore their creative side, and discover a bright burst of confidence when it comes to public speaking. Suitable for stimulating the throat chakra the most because it improves our ability to communicate. It is excellent for instructors and increases the general vibration of health.

Blue Lapis

Blue lapis lazuli has long been associated with deep self-expression and spiritual enlightenment and was a favorite of ancient civilizations. Boost your immune system and prepare ready to use your own inner strength and truth. Using wisdom, spiritual enlightenment, and creativity are the best uses.

Apatite

In terms of the emotional self, apatite's dual-action power promotes lovely social ease and peaceful conversation. It functions as a tonic to bolster the body physically. The best applications are problem-solving, innovative thinking, and effective communication.

Aquamarine

This watery stone is renowned for blending peaceful vibrations with a rush of vitality. It has endless ocean colors, a magnificent ebb and flow, and it brings instant serenity to the heart. Jump straight in as aquamarine tempts you to swim against the ebbing tide rather than sink. Best suited for: quiet reflection, maintaining emotional equilibrium, lucid communication, moments of transformation, and inner resiliency.

Kyanite

A wonderful mover of emotional barriers and a conductor of energy, Kyanite is constantly working to maintain the free flow of pleasant vibes. Best for: calming frayed nerves, discovering self-expression, confidence, establishing connections with others, and dream recall.

Agate

The earthy stone has traveled all the way to us from ancient Babylon. Agate is renowned for being a prosperous, healthy healing amulet and is all about balancing the opposing energies in the world. For balancing polar opposite energies, boosting self-esteem, and providing protection when traveling (particularly in traffic accidents). Pairs nicely with environmentalists, dentists, and dancers. Gives educators and recreation professionals emotional support.

Crystals for Crown Chakra

Lepidolite

A beautiful purple stone whose frequency is said to encourage synchronicity or fortunate coincidence. Because it serves as our portal to greater consciousness, lepidolite is crucial for the crown chakra. When using lepidolite to open the crown chakra, flashy white mica inclusions may be desirable. A deeper or more substantial purple stone will then have a more calming impact, which is perfect for intensifying meditation states.

Selenite

Selenite is renowned for its capacity to purify other crystals' energies. Before treating a patient, reiki therapists frequently utilize selenite for clearing their energy field of any impurities. Selenite has purifying effects in addition to helping one connect with the spiritual world.

Hypersthene

Given its reputation as a stone of clairvoyance and its frequent association with the third eye chakra, hypersthene is also a potent stone for the crown chakra. A great stone for examining and developing consciousness. Because it is thought to assist the beholder in making tough decisions or in finding answers to persistent unanswerable concerns or desires, many refer to Hypersthene as the Answer Stone. Because of this, Hypersthene is also regarded as a stone of manifestation and a potent instrument for realizing one's goals in life.

Apophyllite

The energy of apophyllite, a very uncommon stone, aids in the revelation of interdimensional awareness. This stone is desired for improving inner vision, communicating with one's spirit guides, and channeling divine guidance.

Rutilated Quartz

The quartz's energy is amplified by metallic inclusions. It expands awareness and grounds light energy into the physical body, which awakens the higher mind.

Scolecite

Excellently made, fluffy pillows in the shape of beige feathers. The heart is awakened by the energy of this crystal, which also gives the wearer inner strength, tranquility, deep meditation, and spiritual development. A well-liked stone for slumber and enlightenment practices.

Lapis Lazuli

The stone lapis lazuli represents knowledge and truth. Lapis is incredibly calming, offers insight into mystical realms, and can improve dream work. One of the most valuable stones in history was the lapis; it was inlaid on King Tutankhamun's sarcophagus. Even now, this stone is highly prized. A variety of deep-blue lapis are available, and they are frequently flecked with golden colors produced by pyrite.

White Agate

The energy of white agate helps to balance the soul's positive and negative energy. This brings about harmony, which helps one communicate with their spirit guides and travel through the realm of angels.

After you have the crystals you wish to work with, knowing a little bit about how to use and care for them is helpful. Crystals love to connect, and there are numerous ways to keep these stones active and in sync with all of your aspirations. Learn how to take care of and use your stones.

Recharge Your Crystals

Crystals need to be activated and purified in order to reach their full potential, and they also need to be routinely cleaned in order to keep that potential. Your crystals gather energy as you use them more regularly. Cleaning crystals before and after use is always advised because they absorb energy from everyone who handles them as well as the surroundings.

Both the sun and the moon are excellent for purifying crystals. Placing your crystals outside in the moonlight during a full moon will not only clear your crystals but will also supercharge them as they absorb the incredible force of the moon's energy. Another technique to cleanse your crystals is to expose them to direct sunshine, provided your crystal isn't overly sensitive to light. If your crystals are water safe, you can try placing your stone beneath a cool stream of water for a few minutes to wash any negative energies away as well. Running water is also claimed to neutralize stones.

Healing With Crystals

There are many sweet, small rituals that bring out the finest in your crystals' sublime power, whether you use them to smudge an area or to banish bad energy from a space. You can use crystals in your full moon meditation routines, everyday yoga practice, and when saying your morning affirmations because they feed off the purpose. Varying crystals have different strengths, and this is what truly distinguishes them from one another. Check out the brief and easy instructions below if you're looking for some guidance on which crystal muse will best suit your needs.

Enhance Your sleep. A night of tossing and turning may leave you feeling at best, exhausted, under-energized, and irritated. A healthy amount of sleep is crucial to our healing process because it offers our bodies time to regenerate cells, strengthens our immune systems, and gives our thoughts a break. Rose quartz emits loving energy that aids in physical relaxation and joy. Citrine provides uplifting energy to prevent catastrophizing in the hours before bed. Popular crystal amethyst is all about gentle tranquility. Emotional strain is lessened with moonstone. You can sleep soundly at night thanks to the protection provided by tourmaline and pyrite. Smoky quartz banishes nightmares. Your dreams come true thanks to the labradorite. Chrysoprase eases tension and stress to promote restful sleep.

Tiger's eye gives you a boost that lets you come out of your shell and interact with the outside world. It jumpstarts your confidence. Citrine is a stone of sunny gladness and is constantly prepared to make you feel more upbeat. Jasper awakens chi, a crucial life force energy that gives us a boost of strength to complete the task at hand. You can see clearly with the help of a clear quartz crystal, enabling you to go in the direction you wish to. It increases intent as well.

Improve your concentration. Quartz is a fantastic tool for anyone looking to improve their attention because of its crystal-clear clarity and ability to sweep the cobwebs from your mind. The stone of study is carnelian. It inspires imagination, provides bravery, and boosts vigor and strong motivation. Fluorite enhances physical and mental equilibrium and coordination, which is precisely the center stand you require when focusing on the work at hand. In addition to being a stone that harmonizes, sodalite is also a strong communicator and a fantastic tool for the office because it keeps you calm and focused rather than anxious. Citrine draws brightness and happiness, guiding you out of gloomy situations so you can face your obligations with humor and comfort. The thinking stone lapis lazuli encourages you to sit in wisdom, concentration, and attention.

Gain mental peace. Jade is renowned for its ability to attract money and prosperity, but it is also a wonderful stone for calming a hyperactive mind. The jade's cool touch and constant ability to soothe keeps you breathing deeply. Stress and tension are said to be easily released when wearing rose quartz. This stone opens the heart chakra, allowing compassion and love to fill you to the brim.

According to legend, opal is the stone of joyful dreams. It aids in removing the burden of depression and allows you to enter the spotlight of prayer and meditation.

Blue lace agate quickly calms the body, mind, and spirit. It is a wonderful shade of blue, delicate and full of promise. Another stone with calming energies is amethyst. It distracts you from worrying about trivial matters by reflecting a higher goal and being a soft purple color. The stone of calm slumber is amber. It encourages introspection and mental cleansing, leaving you peaceful and free from any kind of disorder.

COLOR THERAPY

Chromotherapy, often known as color therapy, is a form of treatment that use light and color to address specific physical and mental health conditions. The ancient Egyptians were the first to use this kind of therapy. For therapeutic purposes, they made use of colored glasses and rooms with sunlight. Color therapy has become increasingly popular over the years, although it is still not a common treatment in Western medicine. It is regarded as quackery or pseudoscience by many medical professionals. Color therapy is distinct from color psychology, which is the study of how various hues affect how people behave and perceive things. It is predicated on the untested notion that a person's "energy" and subsequent health can be affected by specific colors. We've all had personal experiences with how color may influence us. Some people's moods are quickly improved by seeing greenery while out for a daily run, or they feel a little better while wearing a favorite yellow outfit. The origins of color therapy can be found in Indian Ayurveda medicine, which holds that specific hues can be used to balance out the chakras in our bodies.

How Color Therapy Can Be Useful

Chromotherapy is regarded as a form of complementary medical care. It has been suggested to be beneficial for a number of conditions, such as:

- Stress, depression, and aggression
- Elevated blood pressure
- Sleep problems
- Anxiety
- Certain types of cancers
- Skin infections

It is crucial to remember that there is little to no proof that color therapy works for any medical condition. The American Cancer Society asserts that there is no scientific evidence to support any claims that using light or color therapy to treat cancer or any other ailment is successful. The use of color therapy alone as an effective treatment for any of these illnesses is not currently supported by research.

While the foundation of color therapy is the idea that most people respond to certain colors with particular feelings, this isn't always the case. The human race is distinct. Different colors can have different effects on different people. Colors that most people find relaxing or tranquil may make certain people anxious or depressed.

Colors To Heal Each Chakra

Chakra healing or balancing can be achieved by working with colors. To promote or activate the flow of an energy center, one can, at the most basic level, match color with that center's related color. Use red, for instance, to activate the energy of the root chakra and to encourage grounding and general vigor; use orange to focus on the second energy center; use yellow for the third, etc.

Red. It is a passionate, warm color that infuses life and elicits vigor. It is the primary color for the root chakra, which is found at the base of the spine. It is the fundamental frequency linked to the planet Earth. The red frequency indicates an individual who is highly confident in all facets of life. The person lives in fear if the red frequency is low. If the red frequency is on the lower side, a suicidal tendency may also be present.

Orange. It signifies the sacral chakra, the chakra of the mind and body, which is situated two to three inches below the navel and is associated with love and happiness. This color is linked to pleasure, sexual reproduction, and adrenal glands. Creativity also decreases if the orange frequency is weak. Low-orange frequency individuals struggle with infertility. Even their water element is weak, and their desire for sexual activity may be declining. On the other hand, if the frequencies are high, there will also be a high level of sexual desire. The color orange is crucial if you want to start something new, be it a project or a new way of life.

Yellow. It stands in for the solar plexus chakra, which is situated between the sternum and the navel. This vibrant and upbeat color can boost immunity, promote intelligence, purify the body and mind, and aid those who are ill to get better. Yellow is a fire- and action-symbolizing color. We lose some of our ability to activate our plans if the yellow frequency is weak. It is because of an unbalanced yellow color's frequency that someone is easily nervous. These people also experience stomach problems.

Green. It is a symbol of the heart chakra. It has a connection to organs, including the heart and lungs. All heart-related difficulties, such as serenity, harmony, calmness, and the absence of love, can be resolved with this color because it is associated with the heart. This color has a reputation for having balanced therapeutic qualities. Low-green frequency individuals tend to be quite reserved. They don't want to socialize. If the frequency is in excess, then the person is called an extrovert. Both introverts and extroverts don't have harmony.

Blue. It is a symbol of the throat chakra. This has to do with metabolism and the thyroid. Any thyroid patient has an unbalanced blue frequency. From a psychological perspective, women make up the majority of those who are ill. Even children today fit within this category. The frequency of the color blue changed during

COVID-19. Domestic abuse has led to more suppression, which reduces the frequency and makes a person weak.

Indigo. It all comes down to vision. Between both eyebrows is the third eye chakra, which it signifies. This is linked to the pituitary gland and affects how much we value ourselves, as well as how clear-headed, wise, and intuitive we are. Children, in particular, benefit from this color since it helps to improve their concentration, focus, and memory. Physical symptoms include issues like headaches and poor vision.

Violet. The crown chakra, present at the top of the head, is symbolized by this color. It is linked to insight, higher consciousness, and awareness. It serves as a bridge between the interior and exterior worlds. When there is a low frequency of the color violet, all those people who wish to meditate may not be able to do so due, and disconnection and preoccupation are to blame. These colors have connections to the neurological and cerebral systems in terms of wellness.

Colors in the Human Body. While using complementary colors to activate a particular chakra can be effective, one can also employ colors to target various biological functions and energy centers all over the body. Here is a list of hues and body parts based on contemporary therapeutic techniques.

- Red: bones and bone marrow
- Orange: gland and adrenals
- Yellow: (golden yellow): nervous system
- Green: lungs, lung tissues
- Blue: etheric body, optimal bodily functions
- Purple: fascia, skin

The conventional chakra system assigns each energy center one of seven primary colors. However, using color to heal offers a vast array of possibilities. It enables us to change from a static depiction of the chakra system to a dynamic interplay of tints that we may use to enhance the body's energy flow.

How to Introduce Colors? If you want to balance your chakras or unblock each of them, you will have to introduce the respective colors into your life. For instance, if you feel that your creativity is fading away, you can introduce the orange color into your life to heal your sacral chakra. This can be done by wearing that color, watching objects with that color, playing with paints, or wearing stones of that color. When selecting chakra healing stones, color coding can help. Here's a chart highlighting the major chakras' colors and their corresponding stones:

Chakra	Color	Stones
Crown	Purple	Amethyst Diamond Quartz, Clear Selenite
Third eye	Indigo	Amethyst Black Obsidian Purple Fluorite
Throat	Blue	Aquamarine Lapis Lazuli Turquoise
Heart	Green	Green Calcite Green Tourmaline Jade Rose Quartz
Solar Plexus	Yellow	Calcite, Orange Citrine Malachite Topaz
Sacral	Orange	Carnelian Citrine Coral Moonstone
Root	Red	Fire Agate Black Tourmaline Bloodstone Tiger Eye Hematite

REIKI

Reiki, a word that derives from the Japanese words "rei" (universal) and "ki" (life energy), has been practiced for thousands of years. Its current form dates back to the early 1920s when the first reiki school and clinic began in Tokyo, Japan. There were already four other forms or "elements" of reiki practiced in Japan as early as the 1800s, ultimately equaling five types of reiki.

Reiki is also practiced in traditional Chinese medicine (TCM). Its focus is on qi, a.k.a. energy, the basic substance of which the world and our bodies are composed. Qi (Chi) is in a state of continuous flux and can sometimes stagnate in our bodies, causing blockages. Reiki, as an energy healing art, reinvigorates the qi in TCM and relieves pain, aches, and stress.

This form of alternative medicine involves the transfer of energy of the universe from the practitioner's palms to the patient. While it is hard to prove its efficacy scientifically, over 1.2 million American adults have tried it, and over 60 hospitals in the United States offer reiki services to their patients alongside traditional Western medicine treatments. Reiki isn't completely mystifying, although its benefits can seem like magic. There are scientific facts behind it. A study from Hartford Hospital, for instance, showed reiki patients experienced reduced fatigue and had improvements in their sleep.

Benefits of Reiki

The primary benefit of reiki is the feeling of balance that occurs after a session. Numerous studies have documented the relief of pain and anxiety. The entire process focuses on breaking through blockages in your personal energy that are causing illnesses and trauma. This balancing of energy brings about benefits such as:

- Accelerating self-healing abilities
- Instilling deep relaxation
- Helping relieve pain
- Complimenting Western medicine practices
- Improving focus
- Lowering heart rate

To become a reiki healer, one should go through two levels of training, then there is additional training to become a reiki master. It is vital to know your practitioner's level of training to reap the maximum benefits.

Practicing Reiki

Use sacred white sage to bless yourself. Native Americans employed sacred white sage for its potent cleansing qualities. It purges harmful energy from your body or your living environment. Smudging is the practice of using sacred white sage to purify a living area or oneself. To smudge a living room, ignite the tip of a bunch of sage with a match or lighter, let the smoke plume, and then use your hand or a feather wand to waft the smoke around the house clockwise from the front door, blessing each thing as you go until you return to the front door. Use your hands to move the smoke toward your body as you smudge it, blessing every area of it, especially the chakras that run along your midline. Say out loud, "I bless my arms, I bless my neck chakra, I bless my chest," and so forth while you do this. As you continue, be careful to periodically tap the stray ashes into a heat-resistant container.

Reiki Precepts

Precepts are a code of practice. They are mantras that reiki practitioners live by and teach to their patients as part of their journey. They encourage individuals to be mindful and reinforce the connection between mind and body. Patients and students are encouraged to repeat these mantras aloud to start and then silently throughout the session for maximum benefits. In essence, these precepts are the entire system of reiki boiled down to five simple concepts. The five reiki precepts are:

- Do not be angry
- Do not worry
- Be grateful
- Work diligently
- Be kind to others

Reiki Techniques

Reiki meditation encourages practitioners, students, and patients to be aware of and responsible for the healing happening before them. It differs from other forms of meditation, which focus on clearing the mind. With reiki meditation, instead of removing the consciousness of everything, you focus on the energy field around and within you. Techniques used in reiki meditation are:

- Zen
- Cleansing
- Center finger
- Chakra focus

This type of meditation sometimes involves drawing reiki symbols to make you more present at the moment.

A hands-on or hands-off healing modality. Reiki is performed by placing the hands or palms lightly on the body or hovering above it to move energy along the seven chakras of the body. Masters use specific hand movements, reiki symbols, and mantras to direct the energy and break through blockages in the flow.

Reiki symbols. Reiki symbols were once held in secrecy and only revealed to students by a master teacher during initiation. There are five symbols in the reiki healing system. Using these symbols activates a patient's energy field and builds it up significantly. Symbols are activated by tracing them onto the body, such as on the third eye and along the chakras.

The five reiki symbols are:

- Cho Ku rei – Power
- Sei Hei ki – Mental/Emotional Harmony
- Hon Sha ze sho nen – Distance Connection
- Dai ko myo – Master Enlightenment
- Raku - Completion

Reiju and attunements. The practitioner performs the reiju ritual while the patient or student sits in a chair. The practitioner will cleanse the energy around the person using a hands-off approach. It provides a space for the student to draw qi through the body.

Reiju is for attuning the student to their new sight with the intent of reminding them of their connection to the earth. A reiju is completed after each level of reiki. It does not include symbols or mantras. The only thing that changes is the student as they grow spiritually with each session. Reiki is one of many forms of TCM that is effective in pain management and treating emotional disorders such as depression and post-traumatic stress disorder. This noninvasive therapy successfully manipulates the body's energy force alone, with other TCM therapies, or in conjunction with a Western approach.

Receiving energy. Any Reiki practice must be initiated by activating your own energy. Keep your eyes closed and inhale deeply many times. Think of the crown of your head opening and a stream of purifying white light streaming from the top of your head into your heart, then out through your arms and hands. Wherever you most need healing, request to be filled up. This will prevent you from providing reiki to a loved one out of an empty cup. As you feel the energy moving, keep breathing; if your thoughts stray or you start to question whether this is actually working, come back to your breath. Consider yourself a conduit for healing. Next, make a prayer or intention to receive healing for good.

Reiki for sleep. Ask a friend or family member to lie down while you place yourself close to their head to perform a Reiki session focused on promoting sleep for them. Visualize your hands, sending a constant stream of healing light into the back of their heads, freeing their minds of whatever pain or discomfort they may have had that day. Ask your loved one to take several rounds of deep breaths and slowly count an inhale of three seconds and an exhale of three to five seconds. Ask them to slowly see their whole day one memory at a time and to thank each memory before letting it go with their breath.

Allow them to drift off as you continue to channel the energy through your palms and send the healing light into their entire body. Imagine the body becoming healed, relaxed, and heavy for a peaceful night's sleep. You can offer this reiki for as long as you want, but between fifteen and thirty minutes is usually enough for them to feel relaxed and peaceful.

Reiki for stress. Often when people have anxiety and stress, they are not breathing properly, and the shortness of breath can cause more stress. In this reiki session, you want to channel energy down the recipient's shoulders and into their body. Spend ten to fifteen minutes placing your hands on their shoulders. Concentrate on inhaling deeply with them and transmitting energy throughout their entire body. This can help people return to their bodies and naturally bring some of the strong mental activity down. If the other person is lying down, you can keep your hands behind their head too, to help them calm down.

Sealing off the energy. After a healing treatment, it's crucial to express thanks, cleanse your body, and close the energy. To cleanse yourself and thank the recipient for the exchange, you can simply take a step back, wipe your hands clean of any extra energy, and place them in prayer. A big circle can also be drawn, with hands clasped in prayer at the end and arms crossed in front of the body to represent the joining of the two forces.

CANDLES GAZING

If you have ever found the sight of a flickering candle flame to be soothing and meditative, you are not alone in this. Do you know that candle gazing, also known as trataka, is a very old practice? Candle gazing meditation entails gazing at a flame and directing your concentration there, as opposed to other types of meditation that involve closing your eyes and turning inside. You may easily add this effective exercise into your daily routine to reap its advantages!

Candle Gazing Benefits

Candle gazing is a fantastic alternative for people who find it difficult to keep their minds from straying, and it can be a highly effective meditation technique. That's because it's simpler to maintain concentration and achieve the goal of transcendental meditation—entering a state of pure awareness—by keeping the eyes open and focusing on a dynamic object. We gain all the typical benefits of meditation from practicing trataka, but hatha yoga traditions also claim that there are various additional advantages, such as:

- Enhances vision/eyesight
- Enhances concentration and memory
- Improves patience and willpower
- Increases productivity
- Soothes the mind and promotes inner peace
- Enhances clarity and decision making
- Offers stress and anxiety relief
- Deepens sleep and helps sleep-related disorders
- Improves intuition

How to do candle gazing?

Like other forms of spiritual healing, you can also practice candle gazing all by yourself. But remember that it is not some random act of watching the candle. Follow these basic steps to harness the true benefits of candle gazing:

Set the space. You cannot expect to concentrate on your candle gazing session with people walking around and talking; you need a quiet and calming place to practice this gazing. Ambiance matters when it comes to spiritual healing. Like any other form of meditation, setting the mood begins with the environment around you. Dim the lights and consider utilizing a Himalayan salt lamp to create a cozy atmosphere in the space. Turn off any electronics and ensure there won't be any interruptions.

Put the candle in front of you. Put your candle on a solid surface away from anything flammable. Keep in mind that you want the candle to be at or near eye level; ideally, use a table rather than the ground.

Light the candle. What I usually do is light an aromatic candle, like my favorite lavender candle, to practice candle gazing. In this way, I employ two spiritual healing techniques—aromatherapy and candle gazing—plus the fragrance of the candle gives my living space a nice smell.

Sit in a comfortable position. Choose a position that is comfortable for you to sit in, then meditate as usual. You might decide to sit on a meditation cushion with a blanket covering you to stay warm. Three to four feet should separate you from your candle.

Stare at the candle. Your goal is to maintain a steady gaze on the candle flame without shifting or blinking. After a while, your eyes may start to tear up, but this is natural. Continue until you are physically unable to maintain your open eyes any longer.

Close your eyes at the end. You might get a mental image of the candle flame when you close your eyes. Try to focus this image on your third eye chakra—the point between your eyebrows. When the vision has vanished completely, open your eyes again and repeat the procedure.

Selecting a candle for gazing. While you can meditate with any candle, choosing candles of a certain color can affect both your meditation and aspects of your personality. You might discover that using a candle of a particular hue while meditating will boost its efficiency, depending on your aims. When purchasing candles, consider the materials used in their manufacture and steer clear of any that may contain harmful materials. Candles made of soy wax or beeswax burn cleaner and longer than other candle varieties. Additionally, you can experiment with using various scents to connect with a specific chakra that you might want to open.

Tips for candle gazing. There are effective measures you can take to make candle gazing a more potent and advantageous activity, but it doesn't have to be difficult. Consider the following advice if you're thinking about starting a trataka practice.

- If you practice during the day, you may want to consider sitting in a room with blackout curtains to block out the sunlight.
- Try to trim your candle wick to increase the lifespan of your candle and keep the flame strong.
- Do not strain your eyes—it is better to keep a soft gaze than to stare.
- It works best at nighttime since you have more control over the lighting levels (but avoid looking at screens).

BOOK 5:

CHAKRA IN THE DIGITAL LANDSCAPE

During the past two decades, reported cases of depression and anxiety have increased exponentially. Psychological disorders, personality disorders, frustration, and stress have been constantly rising. While we all are busy taking care of our physical needs, the spiritual needs of the body are often ignored; in fact, we overlook the negative effects that technology use has on our chakras. All that negative energy, when it stays trapped inside each chakra, induces stress, emotional fatigue, distress, depression, anxiety, anger, frustration, and more. Constantly staring at screens, using mobile phones throughout the day, continuous communication, and working under stressful conditions are all reasons why our chakras remain blocked. And to unblock them, we need to go the extra mile and take all necessary measures to digitally detox ourselves once in a while. If you are willing to do so, then this book has got your back; not only will I tell you about the negative effects of living in this digital world, but I will also provide different ways to prevent those effects. Are you ready?

LIVING IN A DIGITAL LANDSCAPE

When ancient yogis and scholars came up with life force healing techniques, there were no mobile phones and cellphones towers around. The recent expansion of cellular and Internet services, along with the prevalence of electronics around us, has made us live in one giant electromagnetic web. Do you remember how in Books 1 and 4, I repeatedly discussed how the frequencies of colors and elements affect the frequencies of the energies of each chakra? Well, if our energy centers are affected by those subtle radiations, how can we think that the intense radiation coming from electronics all around us would not affect us? The aura is an electromagnetic field of the human body, and when that field interacts with EMF from other sources, it may get disrupted. That is why in today's world, it is important for us to not only recognize the negative effects of the technology around us but also to take extra measures to keep our body's energies protected.

Effects of Electromagnetic Pollution Over Prana (The Life Force)

The problem with EMF is something that, in my opinion, needs to be addressed now because it did not exist thousands of years ago. It appears that young people in particular have quite high readings. Our lives have been made easier in some ways but significantly more complicated in others as a result of our preoccupation with smartphones, laptops, desktop computers, home theater systems, and everything else electronic. This increased intake of EMFs has been linked to inflammation, gastrointestinal problems, thyroid disease, anxiety, and stress, especially in people who are susceptible to them. EMFs should be viewed as a dangerous invader since they interfere with your cellular health (after all, we are all electrical beings). We would observe this has had an impact on the prana (life force) of the body in yoga and Ayurveda.

Your body reacts to electromagnetic fields in a way similar to how it does when exposed to harmful substances or heavy metals because your cell membrane receptors recognize them at very low levels of exposure. This is frequently referred to as oxidative stress, which harms DNA and can be the precursor to cancer and contribute to illnesses including fibromyalgia, chronic fatigue syndrome, and insomnia. Children experience this more than adults do.

Negative Effects of Technology

Nobody contests the benefits of digital technology. It can improve productivity, comfort, and communication. However, because we spend so much time online, we have less time to engage in enjoyable things offline. Also, the time we have to spend with the people we care about is decreasing. Our relationships may suffer as a result. Moreover, a growing corpus of studies is looking into how using digital media and engaging in online activities affects both mental and physical health. Scientists have therefore identified some very serious risks related to continued, excessive technology use. Here is a glance at the most recent studies.

Psychological Effects

The rapid advancement of technology is much to blame for the fact that people are more connected than ever. There is evidence of both the bad impacts of technology and its excessive use, even though some forms of technology may have improved the world. In addition to physical problems like eyestrain and difficulties focusing on crucial tasks, social media and mobile devices can also cause psychological problems. Additionally, they might make more serious medical conditions like depression worse. The harmful effects of excessive technology use may be greater on growing children and teenagers.

Depression and anxiety. A 2016 systematic review's authors talked about the connection between social media and conditions, including depression and anxiety. Mixed findings emerged from their research. On these sites, those who engaged in more positive interactions and received more social support appeared to be less depressed and anxious. The opposite was also accurate, though. Higher levels of despair and anxiety were observed in people who believed they engaged in more unfavorable social interactions online and who were more likely to engage in social comparison.

Insomnia. Technology use right before bedtime may interfere with sleep. This results from the stimulation of the brain by blue light, which includes the light from cell phones, e-readers, and laptops. This blue light is sufficient, according to researchers from a 2014 study, to interfere with the body's normal circadian cycle. This disturbance could make it more difficult for someone to fall asleep or make them feel less alert the next day. People should refrain from using electronic gadgets that emit blue light an hour or two before bedtime to prevent possible negative effects on the brain. As an alternative, try relaxing activities like taking a bath, reading a book, or performing some light stretching.

Effects on Physical Health

Not only has technology use been affecting our minds and emotions, but it has also been seriously harming our physical health as well. It has somehow made our lifestyle more sedentary, and that has caused several harmful effects on our bodies.

Eyestrain. A person can pay attention to technologies like mobile phones, computers, and handheld tablets for extended periods of time. Eye fatigue may result from this. Vision blurring and dry eyes are two signs of digital eyestrain. In addition to causing eye pain, eyestrain can also cause pain in the head, neck, or shoulders. Screen glare, screen brightness, and screen viewing from too close or far away cause bad seating posture and eyesight problems. Regular breaks away from the screen could help to prevent eyestrain. Anyone who experiences these symptoms should get a checkup from an optometrist.

Poor posture.

It's possible that poor posture is a result of how people use their computers and mobile gadgets. Musculoskeletal issues may eventually emerge from this. A "down and forward" posture, which involves leaning forward and looking down at the screen, is one that is encouraged by several technologies. As a result, the neck and spine may experience unduly high pressure. A study in the journal Applied Ergonomics found a five-year association between texting on a phone and neck pain or upper back pain in young adults. The results demonstrated that while some individuals continued to experience persistent symptoms, the effects were mostly transient.

However, some research challenges these conclusions. A 2018 study in the European Spine Journal found that the neck position while texting had no impact on symptoms such as neck pain. This study found that texting or "text neck" has no impact on young adults' neck pain. A lengthy follow-up, however, was excluded from the study. Two more factors that may impact neck soreness are age and level of activity.

A general improvement in body posture and strength in the core, neck, and back may result from correcting posture when using technology. For instance, regularly standing or stretching may assist lessen stress on the body if an individual spends a lot of his time sitting still, such as when working at a desk. Moreover, taking little breaks every hour, such as a quick lap around the office, can keep the muscles relaxed and prevent tension and bad posture.

Reduced level of exercise. Digital technology used in daily life is mostly passive. Using these technologies for an extended period of time increases sedentary behavior, which is known to have detrimental effects on health, including:

- Obesity
- Hypertension
- High cholesterol
- Digestive problems
- Heart disease
- Type 2 diabetes

It may be possible to encourage a more active lifestyle by finding ways to take breaks from sedentary technologies.

Managing Your Online Presence

Do you ever pick up your phone to read the news only to get sidetracked by comments on a post about something you don't even care about? Has doom scrolling made you feel anxious? Do you wake up every night with a kink in your neck from gazing at screens all day? I know what it's like. My first job forced me to spend a great amount of time each day staring at computer and smartphone screens. I've come to realize how important it is to regularly disengage from screens in order to keep my equilibrium and mental tranquility. For me, it all boils down to setting boundaries for time and space. Here are some specific suggestions that I use to limit my screen usage and keep my mental health in check.

Customize your social media feeds. When I understood it was appropriate to unfollow or mute accounts that made me grimace, tighten my jaw, roll my eyes, or just feel "meh," I discovered using social media to be a much more enjoyable experience. On Facebook, Instagram, or Twitter, you can mute someone without worrying that you'll offend them because they won't be aware of it. Just follow the accounts that are publishing stuff you actually enjoy or find helpful.

Control how much news you consume. I can recall a time when reading the morning newspaper and watching the nightly news were the only reliable sources of information. With social media platforms that update every millisecond and twenty-four-hour news cycles, we may be tempted to check for changes all day long. Consider scheduling daily news checks at certain times. Additionally, I find it useful to bookmark and add a few reliable news accounts to a Twitter list so I can just look at the stories from these accounts. Avoid doom scrolling at all costs, as it can frighten you.

Your phone's notifications should be disabled or limited. Is it really necessary to receive an alert informing you that a high school classmate you haven't seen since prom liked the sunset photo you uploaded on Facebook? You'll be less likely to go for your phone if you only set notifications for reminders you actually need, like meetings and birthdays.

Try to stay focused. Throughout the day, our attention is diverted in a number of ways, and our gadgets may only serve to increase this. Your attention is diverted if you are watching TV while concurrently using your phone, tablet, or computer to browse the Internet. Do you think that is a good use of time? Think about using one screen or one activity at a time. It's a great idea to know exactly what you're going to do before using your computer or another gadget. Go for it if what you want to do is to spend an hour curled up on the couch with a cup of tea and checking social media. Avoid repeatedly clicking if your goal is to look up a recipe, but you come across fascinating news or something else that catches your eye. If you're short on time, jot down what interests you and save it for later. (Use paper and a pen, pin it to a Pinterest board labeled "save it for later," use a notes app, or email it to yourself to read later).

When bored or stressed out, avoid watching TV or other screens. Have you ever become disinterested in watching TV and then picked up your phone or tablet to read your email? Have you ever run into a brick wall when working on a project for work and take a break by browsing the Internet? Have you ever had trouble stopping yourself from thinking about something upsetting and looked for comfort on social media? If you want to feel engaged or healthier right now, ask yourself if you actually need screen time. If the answer is no or you're not sure, think about taking a break without a screen. If you're anything like me, going for a walk around the block, turning on some music, or doing some grounding meditation would be more beneficial.

Avoid using electronics while eating. You can establish a rule in your household prohibiting the use of electronic devices at the table. Live alone? Use the same standard. To fight temptation, switch to silent mode. Use this guideline when eating lunch in front of your computer as well. Try to plan your day so that you can set aside uninterrupted time to eat.

Avoid using your phone while interacting with others. I frequently turn my phone to silent or airplane mode while I'm with friends or family so I can focus entirely on them. I also try to avoid using it unless I'm taking pictures.

Select a time each day to tune in and out. It may appear that you have more free time for the activities you lose out on, on hectic days when you set aside hours that are screen free. From 9 p.m. until 8 a.m., I like to leave my mobile phone in "do not disturb" mode. I try to cease using electronics one to two hours before bedtime, or I limit their use to listening to music, podcasts, or audiobooks. The blue light they emit can be disruptive to sleep. I also lower the blue light on my phone and computer using the "night shift" setting.

Consider screen time substitutes. Consider how much time you actually spend online before you whine that there is not much time in the day to exercise, spend time with friends and family, take a break for a meal, or rest. The next time you reach out to passively ingest a never-ending stream of blurry photographs, stop and take a different path. Make a call to a loved one, dance along to your favorite music, or decide to engage in a self-care activity that makes you feel wonderful. If you find satisfaction in other, more meaningful pursuits, cutting back on screen time may be simpler for you. The more screen time you cut back on, the more time you'll have for the things (and people!) you feel like you're missing. It can be quite beneficial to spend even five minutes offline.

Digital Clearing and Shielding Processes

In order to protect yourself from the negatives of the technology around you, you will need a digital detox. You can cleanse your aura of the harmful electromagnetic fields around you by avoiding the use of technology, including social media, smartphones, televisions, computers, and tablets. It's common to think of detoxing from digital devices as a method to concentrate on in-person social interactions without interruptions. People can release the stress brought on by continual connectivity by temporarily giving up their digital devices. Consider some of the possible advantages and techniques of performing a digital detox before deciding if it is appropriate for you.

Being online and fully immersed in the digital world is merely a part of daily life for many individuals. The average American adult spends about 11 hours per day reading, watching, or engaging with media. There are a variety of reasons you might wish to temporarily put down your phone and other electronic gadgets. Without the distractions that your phone and other devices cause, you might enjoy some alone time. In other situations, you can feel that your excessive technology use is making your life too stressful. In a survey by the group

Common Sense Media, 50 percent of teenagers said they believed they were dependent on their mobile devices. A staggering 78 percent of the teenagers who responded to the survey claimed they checked their electronic gadgets hourly.

Performing a Digital Detox

In today's digital world, in which we cannot practically function without the use of technology, we cannot simply switch off all the devices or start living in the woods—we cannot survive in this way! That is why we need to exercise an approach that will both be practical and feasible for all of us.

Your mental health can benefit from removing yourself from technology but engaging in a digital detox doesn't require total withdrawal from your phone and other tech connections. Setting boundaries and ensuring that you are using all the electronic devices in a way that benefits, rather than harms, your emotional and physical health are usually more important aspects of the process.

Be practical. If you can go completely offline for a period of time, it might be something that you want to try. Some people may find it freeing and reviving to be fully cut off. Many people may not be able to entirely give up all digital contact, especially if they absolutely need to keep connected for jobs, education, or other obligations. This is not to say that you cannot benefit from a digital detox; the trick is to make disconnecting a part of your daily routine and way of life.

If your employment requires you to use your devices all day, consider performing a mini-detox at the conclusion of the workday. Decide on a time when you want to switch off your gadgets, then concentrate on having a night without using social media, texting, watching online videos, or engaging in any other technological distractions.

Set limits. While complete disconnection isn't always possible or even desirable, placing boundaries on when these digital connections can encroach on your time can be beneficial for your mental health. Setting your phone to airplane mode will ensure that you are not interrupted by phone calls, texts, other messages, or app notifications while working out, for instance, if you want to use it to play your Spotify or Apple Music playlist. Setting restrictions on the kinds and times of connections you'll make can help you keep your real-world activities free from interruptions from the digital world. Other circumstances in which you might want to restrict your use of digital devices include:

- When you eat meals, especially when you're dining with others
- After you get up in the morning or when you go to bed
- When pursuing a project or a hobby
- While you are among friends or family
- Each night before you go to sleep

According to research, using social media for no more than thirty minutes a day can dramatically boost well-being and lessen depressive and lonely symptoms.

It may be beneficial to limit your use of mobile devices right before bed. According to one evaluation of the literature, using media devices was associated with unsatisfactory sleep, insufficient sleep, and excessive daytime drowsiness. Instead of playing on your phone while lying in bed, try spending some time reading a book or magazine before bed.

Remove distractions. Turning off push notifications on your phone is another method to begin your digital detox. Every time you receive a message, mention, or new post, social media apps and news websites send you an alert. Instead of clicking the link every time you receive a notification, schedule a specific time each day to check your messages or mentions. Then set a specific period of time, perhaps twenty or thirty minutes, to catch up and send replies. You may discover that leaving your phone behind, if only for a little while, is beneficial.

Make it work for you. Here are a few ideas you might want to try:

- **Digital Fast:**
  - Try putting away all of your electronic devices for a day or up to a week.
- **Recurrent Digital Detox:**
  - Decide which day of the week you will be device free.
- **Targeted Detox:**
  - Focus on limiting your usage of a troublesome app, website, game, or digital tool if it consumes an excessive amount of your time.
- **Social Media Detox:**
  - Concentrate on limiting or perhaps quitting using social media for a certain amount of time.

Tips:

Some people find it quite easy to give up their electronics. Others will find it far more challenging and occasionally even anxiety-inducing. You can take the following steps to make sure your digital detox is more successful:

- Inform your loved ones that you are taking a digital detox and ask for their assistance and support.
- Find ways to stay distracted and keep other activities on hand.
- Delete social media apps from your phone to reduce temptation and easy access.
- When you are tempted to use your gadget, consider leaving the house and going somewhere else, such as out to dinner with friends or on a stroll.
- Maintain a journal to record your progress and share your reflections on the experience.

It is obvious that minimizing screen time is important for maintaining our health and well-being. Moreover, it is the duty of parents to shield their kids and teenagers from an excessive amount of digital media. As a result, parents must establish explicit rules for their children's usage of technology then enforce those rules with suitable penalties. Children are rarely motivated to unplug, unlike adults, who may find an internal drive to do so. On their screens, they want to stay connected to their social networks, entertainment, and diversions. Therefore, aiding children in their digital media detox may require some effort and planning.

Attend a digital detox retreat. Retreats for digital detoxification can be helpful for families. As a result, the entire family travels to a brand-new location, and everyone makes a commitment to largely or entirely avoiding technology. It could be for a single day, several days, a week, or longer. The use of phones keeps us indirectly unaware of what is happening around us. Therefore, unplugging creates additional chances for family time. We are also more prone to directly interact with our surroundings.

Start slow. A complete getaway is not necessary for a digital detox. Doing brief digital detoxes throughout the day is an additional choice. Don't glance at your phone for fifteen minutes on the first day. Unplug for thirty minutes the following day or take several fifteen-minute breaks. Every week, put in up to a half or full day of work on avoiding social media and digital media.

Maintain parts of the home that are off limits to screens. Make a screen- and scroll-free zone out of your bedroom or another area of your house. This could include the kitchen in addition to the dining room. Families can also establish a room that is just used for board games and reading. Kids are also more likely to engage in outside play if technology is prohibited. Moreover, children don't require computers in their bedrooms. They may use a family computer if they are using it for their homework or any other approved screen time. The location of this computer in the home allows parents to keep an eye on what the children are doing online and for how long. I have a rule that says I can't read the news in bed so I can relax before going to sleep.

Plan family activities without technology. Visit a children's museum, join a parent-child circus, or enroll younger children in an art class. Ropes courses, rafting, snowboarding, or dance lessons could be appealing to teenagers. Or simply take everyone on a hike or a swim outside. Exercise and exposure to the environment also help kids avoid using their phones and have significant positive effects on their mental and physical health. In one Mind study, 95 percent of people surveyed claimed that putting down their phones to spend time outside improved their mood. They changed their negative and anxious feelings to ones that were more peaceful and balanced. Inform children about the negative effects of screen time and digital media on their bodies and minds. Don't undervalue their capacity to weigh the advantages and disadvantages. Knowledge alone might not change their behavior because technology has a great hold over them. However, they will comprehend the significance of digital detox. It is a plan for protection and prevention rather than a sanction.

Reconnect to Nature

I would like to end this book on this one note: Reconnecting to nature is our only way to be truly healthy. Our bodies were created to harness the energy of sunlight, take benefit of fresh fruit, enjoy different weather, roam in green fields, and connect to the earth. The more concrete hubs we've created, the more we are getting away from nature. We are practically living in a virtual world where most of our time is spent interacting with people over screens and living behind closed doors. Remember, the energy flowing through us is part of the universal energies, and if we don't let it connect to the universe in its own natural way, we will end up blocking our energy centers, and that is exactly what has been happening these days. Everyone seems more frustrated, more agitated, and more confused even though we are provided with all the comfort in the world. It is only because we are depriving ourselves of the spiritual strength we need. Now, I am not saying to abandon your home and start living woods because, at this point, it is not practical, but there are several things we can do while continuing with our current lives:

Wherever you are, seek out nature! Around us, there is nature. It could be a garden, a nearby park, a beach, or open terrain. There are community gardens or courtyards to discover and explore, even in cities where it can be more difficult to find nature. On your way out for the early shift, be on the lookout for an urban fox, any changes in the weather, or chirping outside your window. Wherever you are, try to take in the natural world in whatever way speaks to you.

Embrace nature with all of your senses! Your mental health might benefit greatly from taking some quiet time in nature to ponder while engaging all of your senses. Try listening to bird music, keeping an eye out for bees and butterflies, or observing the movement of the clouds, whether you're relaxing in the yard or on your way to work. You can discover peace and joy by taking advantage of all of these wonderful aspects of nature.

Experiencing nature. Try to spend as much time as you can in green environments, such as parks, gardens, or forests, or in blue spaces, such as the beach, rivers, and wetlands. This can improve your mood, lower your risk of mental health issues, and make you feel better about things. If venturing outside seems intimidating, consider going with a friend or family member or selecting a familiar location.

Let nature come to you! Due to factors like where you live, how busy you are, how safe you feel, or your health, it might be difficult to go to natural areas. Why not try bringing some of the outside inside? Pots of herbs from the grocery store are an excellent place to start if you want to have something natural to see, touch, and smell in your home. Consider how to maximize any gardens, allotments, or balconies you may have. Get a bird feeder, grow some flowers, plants, or vegetables, and observe your surroundings. If you're not into gardening, you can still interact with nature through literature, visual arts, and audio recordings.

Exercise around nature. Try to exercise outside if you are physically able to do so, whether it's a quick stroll, cycle, or run. Getting outside and exercising in the fresh air may help prevent or lessen negative emotions like rage, fatigue, and melancholy. Unless you're listening to nature sounds, try leaving the headphones at home. Or why not explore new paths that take you closer to natural areas or bodies of water?

Couple nature with creativity. Consider merging your natural surroundings with your creative spirit. By capturing the terrain, flora, or animals in words, pictures, drawings, or paintings, you can deepen your sense of connection. This could also entail engaging in creative pursuits outside of the classroom, such as dancing, music, or art. You can feel better and experience less stress by doing all of these things. You can find meaning and a lasting emotional connection to nature by appreciating its beauty and using your creativity to convey it.

Protect and preserve nature. Giving something attention can be a really wonderful way to feel good. And what better thing to preserve than the natural world? Nature is extremely amazing; try your best to preserve it through your choices and actions. Recycling, walking instead of driving, or even joining local conservation or clean-up groups can all help. Maintaining nature might give you the impression that you're doing your part, which can boost your mood in general.

OVERVIEW OF SEVEN CHAKRAS

Chakra	Sanskrit name	Color	Location	Element
Root Chakra	Muladhara	Red	Base of spine	Earth
Sacral Chakra	Svadhistana	Orange	Below the belly button	Water
Solar plexus Chakra	Manipura	Yellow	Upper abdomen	Fire
Heart Chakra	Anahata	Green	Middle of the chest	Air
Throat Chakra	Visshudha	Blue	Throat	Space/Ether
Third eye Chakra	Ajna	Indigo	Between the eyebrows	Light
Crown Chakra	Sahasrara	Violet	Top of the head	None

CONCLUSION

We cannot deny the existence of energies flowing within us and in the universe. Matter itself is a physical form of those energies. Like elements, we human beings also absorb and radiate energies, and for the sake of our spiritual and physical well-being, the flow of negative energies out of the body and the flow of positive energies into the body is quite important. While different people associate yoga, meditation, and the concept of healing energies with different religions, faith, or theologies, none can deny the benefits of all of them. Your mind and body are both connected to one another and all your senses; by focusing on exercises that will help create a stronger connection within, you can truly discover your inner strength.

Though chakra is a word we have all have heard, the complete philosophy behind the chakra systems and how they work is not the kind of information we come across every day. All those mood swings, irritation, frustration, anxiety, and depression we usually suffer might be caused by any of our blocked chakras. So, we need to know how a blocked chakra manifests itself and the different ways to unblock them. Being a yoga practitioner myself, I have been digging deep into the unseen world of chakras for more than fifteen years. I was introduced to the concept of prana or qi when I was quite young, and since then, my family and I have been using all forms of healing remedies and rituals to cleanse ourselves. I know it is difficult to detox our minds and body from negative energies, living in this digital age with so much going on in our lives. So, keeping all those facts in mind, I compiled this *Chakra Healing Bible.*

I hope after reading all the different parts of these books, you will become more aware of the power of your chakras, and all the healing methods will leave you feeling spiritually, emotionally, and physically stronger, calmer, and more contented than ever before.

REFERENCES

AFL Team March 6, 2020N. C. », September 30, 2022, October 5, 2022, August 25, 2022, July 4, 2012, & March 30, 2012. (2021, December 8). 10 tips for managing screen time. Active For Life. Retrieved October 25, 2022, from https://activeforlife.com/10-tips-to-manage-screen-time/

Amoosbrugger. (2021, September 2). Chakra-balancing yoga sequence. Yoga Journal. Retrieved October 25, 2022, from https://www.yogajournal.com/practice/yoga-sequences/7-poses-chakras/

Bertone, H. J. (2019, October 2). Which type of meditation is right for you? Healthline. Retrieved October 25, 2022, from https://www.healthline.com/health/mental-health/types-of-meditation

Chakra balancing treatment. A Touch of Beauty - beauty salon in Goodwood. (n.d.). Retrieved October 25, 2022, from https://atouchofbeauty.com.au/blog/article2/chakra-balancing-treatment/

Complete guide to 7 chakras & their effects: Arhanta yoga blog. Arhanta Yoga Ashrams. (2022, October 8). Retrieved October 25, 2022, from https://www.arhantayoga.org/blog/7-chakras-introduction-energy-centers-effect/

Johnson, C. (2022, September 15). Chakra meditation. Unblock The 7 Chakras with Guided Meditation. Retrieved October 25, 2022, from https://www.anahana.com/en/meditation/chakra-meditation

Nikos, Ramteke, A. K., Burgin, T., Donnell, J., maxwell, W., Petchiram, Pradhan, A., Dane, Goyal, S., Morris, M., & Daniel. (2021, June 16). Understanding the flow of Prana (life-force energy). Yoga Basics. Retrieved October 25, 2022, from https://www.yogabasics.com/learn/the-flow-of-prana/#:~:text=Prana%20can%20be%20translated%20from,us%20and%20inside%20of%20us.

Philosophy of yoga. Yoga Basics. (n.d.). Retrieved October 25, 2022, from https://www.yogabasics.com/learn/philosophy-of-yoga/

Shah, P. (2020, November 12). A Primer of the Chakra System. Chopra. Retrieved October 25, 2022, from https://chopra.com/articles/what-is-a-chakra

Stelter, G. (2016, December 19). Chakras: A beginner's guide to the 7 chakras. Healthline. Retrieved October 25, 2022, from https://www.healthline.com/health/fitness-exercise/7-chakras

Stokes, V. (2021, October 25). *Feeling ungrounded? your Root Chakra may need some love. Healthline.* Retrieved October 25, 2022, from https://www.healthline.com/health/mind-body/root-chakra-healing

Team, M. (2021, May 14). *What is Chakra Meditation?: What are the chakras? Mindworks Meditation.* Retrieved October 25, 2022, from https://mindworks.org/blog/chakra-meditation/

The Times of India. (2019, August 9). *What are the 7 chakras in our body? here is a complete breakdown of - times of India. The Times of India.* Retrieved October 25, 2022, from https://timesofindia.indiatimes.com/life-style/health-fitness/home-remedies/what-are-the-7-chakras-in-our-body-here-is-a-complete-breakdown/articleshow/70605207.cms

What is chakra therapy? Dr Deb Therapy. (2021, September 17). Retrieved October 25, 2022, from https://drdebtherapy.com/what-is-therapy/what-is-chakra-therapy/#:~:text=Chakra%20therapy%20focuses%20on%20clearing,that%20help%20balance%20each%20chakra.

Yogicameron. (2022, September 20). *Everything you've ever wanted to know about the 7 chakras in the body. mindbodygreen.* Retrieved October 25, 2022, from https://www.mindbodygreen.com/articles/7-chakras-for-beginners

Made in United States
Orlando, FL
25 August 2023

36415175R00091